Following the

to the Ultimat

ABSOLUTE TRUTH

Robert B Palaszewski

ABSOLUTE TRUTH

Published by ATP Ministry Press

Through the International Localization Network Inc and

Five Stones publishing.

www.ilncenter.com

www.atpministry.com

First Edition Published December 2017

ISBN: 978-1-945423-07-9

Cover Design: Nicole Barnum

Published in the United States of America

DEDICATION

This work is dedicated to all the "TRUTH" seekers, who honestly and genuinely search for the Ultimate Source of all reality.

ACKNOWLEDGMENTS

Sometimes I feel as if presenting any work as your own is somehow intellectually dishonest. So much of the labor and toil and sweat equity of others goes into producing even the most modest offerings. What can I offer that others have not offered first? So perhaps we bring our own 'take' on the matter; our own organization of thought.

It was the work of CS Lewis and Ravi Zacharias that guided so much of my early thinking in this area. Then there is Lee Strobel, the late Grant Jeffrey, Josh McDowell, Norman Geisler, Frank Turek, Dr William Craig, Dr Philip Johnson, Chuck Missler, S Michael Houdmann and Del Tackett & Dr Stephen Meyer of the Truth Project. And I know I'm missing others. Thanks to all of these for doing the heavy lifting and original thinking.

TABLE OF CONTENTS

FORWARD

"Belief determines behavior." I can't remember where I heard or read this, but it's certainly not original. While it may not be original, it is true! We do what we do…or not, because of what we believe. Have you ever driven 40mph in a 30mph zone? Why? Why do we do it? Because we believe nothing will happen, or nothing will happen that we can't handle…with keen eyesight and cat-like reflexes. We break the laws of the land because somehow, we believe they don't apply to us. They are for someone else in another context altogether.

As quiet as it is kept, belief is a wonderfully powerful gift to us from the Father. What we choose to believe in is the issue. For the true believer, I want to be careful with the use of the word "Christian," as it has become a kind of catch all, anything goes, in vogue word in our culture. But for the believer, there is a God and we behave as such. You see the biblical world-view is a world-view that is based on the belief that there is a sovereign God, unmatched and without rival.

I will not attempt to delve into the aspects of world-views, the piece you're about to read can and will by far better explain what a world-view is and the many competing world-views out there. However, by definition, a world-view is a term to describe the belief system by which a person understands or makes decisions about the world. A biblical Christian world-view, is one that has Jesus Christ as its cornerstone!

With all the world-views out there, let me ask you a few questions; do you know in whom you believe? Do you know why you believe? Is your belief reflected in your daily decision making? This book will help you sort through the above questions. Not only will it help you sort through them, this book will bring you face to face with The Sovereign God!

Let me try to wrap up my thoughts, around this final point. If there is a rub with those of us who have or are supposed to have a Biblical Christian World-view it is this. What we say we believe is not readily evident in what we do, in what we say, where we go or what we buy! I contend that the "irresistible witness" of the first century church was in fact, that her members lived out their newfound faith. What they believed governed every decision they made. As a result, they were amazingly different from those around them. Not different peculiar, but different in peace, security, gentleness, patience, well you get the picture. You see, to be a witness is not just to tell your story, but it is to live yielded to and governed by the one who saved us. It is to have one's behavior determined by one's belief. For those of us who name the name of Jesus herein lies our "irresistible witness."

As you work your way through the pages of this book, I pray that the Father would bring you face to face with who He is. It is only then that you can have a clear image of who you are and how you are to live in this world. May you say as the Apostle Paul said, "I know in whom I have believed…" and may what you believe determine everything you do!

Pastor William T. Clark Jr.

PART I
THE VERDICT OF REASON

INTRODUCTION

Why do you believe? Or perhaps the question should be: Why don't you believe? The question of 'Faith,' of 'World-view,' of true 'Belief,' is the most essential question faced by every human being who has ever lived and reached the age of reason. It starts with the simple – but not very easy question: Does God exist? If He does: Who is He? As a Christian I believe that the answer is plain and that it is revealed in the Bible. But this is no leap in the dark; no exercise in blind and unreasoned faith. Anyone who has taken the time to study the Bible realizes that it is a book of truth claims. History, prophecy, moral law and miraculous testimony all laid out and ready to be tested. Claiming to be the very Word of God it sets a high standard and begs to be challenged.

In this book we will set out the evidence – and it is ample - for both the existence of God and most specifically for the Christian notion of who God really is. In testing the evidence, we will explore the nature of Truth itself, examine the question of good and evil, and inexorably follow the trail of reason, science, and the history that rationally leads to a call to put our faith in Jesus Christ as the promised Messiah of the Jewish tradition. It is a journey to the heart through the window of the mind. Believer or sceptic, I invite you to take the challenge and come along for the ride.

FRAMING THE QUESTION

Let's begin with what the world believes. This could be their credo. Let us begin by stating the obvious. No modern, no post-modern thinking person can deny it. Science stands triumphant! We have mapped the human genome, we are exploring space, and are on the threshold of cloning copies of ourselves. Man is fast overthrowing the ancient idols of external morality and superstition. This is the 21st century. The old truth no longer applies. There is nothing but the DNA. We are but a cosmic accident, products of nothing plus chance. Therefore, we owe no allegiance outside ourselves. God is chance. He is accident. He is the great Nothing. God is dead. The very notion of God is dead. We are free to remake ourselves in any image we want. We are free. We are masters of our own souls. So all truth is illusion. It is a reflection of the nothing. It is our own to create. Truth, in the higher, ultimate sense is false. All is truth, because it is ours. Everything, everyone is subject to auto-interpretation. There is nothing outside to tell us the right and the wrong. There can be nothing higher than ourselves, we accidents of nature. We are become our own gods.

This has become the mission statement of our age. It is the assertion of man's supremacy and God's demise. So many of the denizens of science, high priests of our culture, declare it so. Who are we to question? Yet God's fingerprints lie all around us. The universe is filled with astounding evidence of His design. We see it in the workings of the heavens, in the delicate life supporting balance of our own planet. Science now believes there may be as many as 100 billion to 200 billion galaxies out there, with tens of millions of stars in even the smallest ones.1 Then how many planets exist? How many atoms are there in the universe? We find evidence in the precise workings of each atom, in each element, in each substance of nature. We witness it in the harmony and power of that nature, and in the functioning of the animal kingdom. If we listen, we can hear the evidence in our heart. Some things are immoral. We just know this. That murder is evil is little debated. That lying and stealing and cruelty and unfairness are wrong is an accepted principal. What makes this so? And we see it in the nature of love. It is evident in the love of parent for child, in the other-centeredness of love between a man and woman, and in the self-sacrifice sometimes found among comrades in war.

While many may mock or discount the evidence, the Bible itself holds us responsible for this understanding. In his letter to the Church at Rome, the Apostle Paul wrote: *"For the wrath of God is revealed from heaven against all ungodliness and unrighteousness of men, who suppress the truth in unrighteousness, because what may be known of God is manifest in them, for God has shown it to them."* (Romans 1:18-19) And just how does this evidence manifest? "For since the creation of the world His invisible attributes are clearly seen, being understood by the things that are made, even His eternal power and Godhead, so that they are without excuse." (Romans 1:20) So much for the evidence of creation. Just a little later in this epistle, Paul makes the argument of conscience. We are to understand that God exists even by the internal evidence of conscience put within us. *"for when Gentiles, who do not have the law, by nature do the things in the law, these, although not having the law, are a law to themselves, who show the work of the law written in their hearts, their conscience also bearing witness, and between themselves their thoughts accusing or else excusing them)."* (Romans 2:14-15)

There is so much evidence out there to be examined without even going to a scripture confirmed by history. Yet there are many that will not see, that refuse to believe. There seems to be a will to disbelieve. Perhaps it is the loss of control entailed in that act. To believe would mean that one would no longer be at the center of one's personal universe. The notion of God means submission. To the self-immersed this can be a terrifying and revolting experience. It means the existence of a power greater than one's self. If true, it means a Truth that transcends all others, by which all things are judged.

In this book we'll examine the evidence and put it to the test. Sometimes this will be a systematic approach – and at other times it may seem more random. But we will explore what we know and what we can know. Having studied this for years I hope that you will find with me that the evidence for the biblical world-view is all around us. It can be found in the design and scope of the universe, the morality found in the hearts of men, and the very existence of love. The evidence for Jesus is comprehensive. It is apparent in the accuracy of the gospels confirmed by its' agreement with earlier scripture, independent historical sources, and archaeological finds. Then there is the testimony of dozens of fulfilled Old Testament Prophecies. Perhaps most compellingly, there is the fact that his companions believed so completely in His resurrection that they all put their lives on the line to spread its truth. With nothing material to gain, not one recanted as they faced torture and death. Finally there are the millions of lives that have been touched and changed by faith in Christ. Whether you are looking to deepen your understanding of the faith – or – you are a skeptic challenging the Christian world-view, I hope that you will join us for the journey. Take the challenge of truth and reason….and see where it leads.

CHAPTER 1
WORLD-VIEWS & "TRUTH"

In order to even begin to tackle the subject of faith and bridge the deep divisions that divide our world we need to find a common language between atheist, skeptic, Hindu, Muslim, New Ager and Christian. But it seems that certain irreducible barriers exist. While some are on a search for 'Truth' – many of this post-modern generation will tell you that 'Truth' doesn't exist – or that all views are 'True' – it is but a product of individual choice. So how do we have this conversation at all?

WORLD-VIEWS & "TRUTH"

We'll start with this: We all have a world-view. It comes with the territory of living. But since a lot of folks might be unfamiliar with the term we need start with a definition. I would describe a world-view as a 'Theory of Everything.' It is our view of how ….. and why everything operates. The American Scientific Affiliation defines it thus. "A world-view is a theory of the world, used for living in the world. A world view is a mental model of reality — a framework of ideas & attitudes about the world, ourselves, and life, a comprehensive system of beliefs — with answers for a wide range of questions."[2] It especially answers the big questions: Is there a God? What's He like? Is there purpose in life? And what is the meaning of life. In some sense, our world-view will be wholly personal; in others it will fall into broad patterns defined by religious or philosophical orientation. It of course will be fed by our rational interpretation of events. But it will also be influenced by what we are taught, by our fears – and by our prejudices. There are millions that rarely if ever challenge their world-view – and others in which it has become so ingrained that no amount of "Truth" will move them to a more reasonable position. Still others believe that it is merely a matter of preference and choice. They argue that no one religion or philosophy can have the full "Truth." So they all must have a piece of it. These conclude that all ways lead to the same place anyway. [This is but a comforting exercise in illogic, as we will argue later.]

Among philosophers who study such things, it is generally held that a world-view must answer five essential questions.

Origin: Where did we come from?

Identity: Just who are we?

Meaning: (The 'Why are we here?' question)

Morality: How are we to live?

Destiny: Where are we headed when this life is all done?

And the most important factor in determining our answers to those questions depends on whether God does or does not exist. It is the essential question.[3] So let's unpack the four basic world-views. Each will answer these questions in a different way.

THEISM: God exits and He is an eternal and self-existent Being

MATERIALISM: Matter and energy and the laws of nature are the ultimate reality. They define and determine everything. As Carl Sagan put it: "The cosmos is all there is or ever was or ever will be."

DEISM: God exists. But He doesn't interfere in His creation. He just lets it run any-old-way it will. Good luck to ya!

PANTHEISM: God is a Force. This Force is NOT rational, NOT conscious. And most importantly, the physical world – the cosmos – is all a part of this god. And so are we. The conclusion: We are therefore, in a sense, divine beings ourselves. (How convenient!)[4]

By way of illustration let's just look at how two of these world-views answer the five big questions. The Materialist would make the case that our Origin was just one big cosmic accident. That means that our Identity could only be defined as the animal products of natural forces; a higher form of cosmic goo, if you will. With that as our Origin and Identity it logically follows that there is no higher Purpose for our existence. So we may institute the Morality we choose for a Purpose of our own determination – because we have no real Destiny. Our Destiny is .....well, nothingness. By way of comparison let's look at the Theistic world-view – and narrow that down even further to the Biblical / Christian variety. Our Origin is from God. In fact, in Genesis, God said: *"Let Us make man in Our image, according to Our likeness."* (Genesis 1:26) So we have the imprint of Divine DNA somewhere in our fallen nature. As to our Identity, John 1:12 tells us we have the "right to become children of God, to those who believe in His name." So our Purpose then is to serve the Living God, our Creator and Father. And it is His perfect nature that becomes the basis for our Morality. We are to *"love the LORD your God"* with our heart, soul, strength and mind. (Luke 1:27) And our Destiny becomes eternal life with Him. Quite the contrast!

But the question should be – not which world-view we prefer – but rather which more perfectly conforms to reality. And that is where we stumble up against the notion of absolute "Truth." You see there is this notion going about that everyone can have their own 'truth.' That there is no overriding "Truth." I remember first encountering it when I read Grapes of Wrath by John Steinbeck. Somewhere in there a character talks about something being "true for him." In other words, it promoted the notion that "Truth" could be specific to the individual. When I was in my teens, that sounded very deep of course. But upon further review, it is logically impossible. You see, the existence of 'objective truth' – is important – because "Truth" – reality, if you will has consequences. What if I'm wrong in my religious beliefs. What if Islam is the only way. Then I, as a Christian would have made a fatal miscalculation and sentenced myself to an eternity in Hell. So it becomes a very pragmatic thing to ascertain and believe only those things that are actually – and objectively – True. But how do we find this "Truth." Can we believe the holy books? OK, then which one? The Bible gives us one set of truths, the Koran another contradictory explanation of reality. Then there's the teachings of Buddha and Hinduism – and we've only scratched the surface of truth-claiming philosophies. But we are looking for a philosophy in the classical sense; one that is rational and supported by the evidence and seeks to find "Truth" through science, evidence and logic.[5]

Now before we go on we've got to understand one thing: We can't even have an argument about whose right about things if we think that "Truth" is relative. We've often seen or heard it said by 'intellectual types' that 'All truth is relative,' or 'There are no absolutes.' But these are actually self-defeating statements. All truth is relative? Well is that a relative truth or an absolute truth? There are no absolutes? Now, is that an absolute truth? Here are some of the real facts about Truth.

Truth is Discovered. It does not depend on us knowing about it.

Truth is True across cultures.

Truth Does Not Change when our beliefs change.

All TRUTH is Absolute! As Geisler and Turek put it in their book I Don't Have Enough Faith to Be an Atheist: "Contrary beliefs are possible, but contrary truths are not possible."[6]

Simple logic tells us that all of this is so. Yet so much of the world tries to argue the fact. It is not a fallacy limited to our modern day and age. The Gospel of John records an exchange between Pontius Pilate and Jesus on the matter. Jesus had just told the Roman Procurator *"You say rightly that I am a king. For this cause I was born, and for this cause I have come into the world, that I should bear witness to the truth. Everyone who is of the truth hears My voice."* Pilate replied: *"What is truth?"* (John 18:37, 38) It was a question dripping with scorn and skepticism, not a serious inquiry on Pilate's part. And how very presciently it anticipated the post-modern mindset. What is truth? The existentialist question screams at us individually and corporately, across the noise and clutter of a culture, pregnant with much knowledge and so little wisdom. It is a question so supremely important, yet very seldom considered by the person too enamored of the world, or preoccupied by success, or self-gratification. Often, when it is considered, it is investigated in a superficial manner, imperfectly applying the principles of rationality and logic or being sidetracked by the irrelevancies of fairness, political correctness, or 'tolerance' as popularly defined. What is truth? We are often a society that little cares, consumed as we are by our toys and indulgences.

Still others are trapped by the alluring notion of 'Tolerance' as the supreme ethic. Some will say: 'There is no absolute truth in religion.' And by that standard might not all religious beliefs be valid? The climate of unquestioning tolerance would have us believe they could be. Who are we to judge one over another? Our culture speaks again. There is no absolute truth. It is the era of the subjective. Each individual is entitled to his own specific truth. 'If you believe it, it is true for you.' It is the reign of relativism. This tolerance has come to mean unqualified and unquestioning acceptance. To judge is evil. Even to judge evil is evil. Our culture allows little in the way of discernment. Everything is to be accepted at face value as what it claims to be. And those who take a biblical view of social issues are labeled as intolerant, homophobic and mean spirited. It cannot be otherwise if there is no objective truth on which to base judgment. All judgment is to be filtered through the self. After all, it all involves personal choices. And who are we to judge? After all 'It's all good'!

Logic tells us this can't be so. Our experience confirms it. Evil is still going to be evil. Murder is always wrong. Good is still good. No matter how some of our intellectual elite may argue to the contrary, there is some transcendent morality, even if the bar has been lowered. Across cultures and time, man senses this within. It is historical fact that not all behaviors are morally equivalent. Prostitution, stealing, murder and adultery are in no way equivalent to sex with love, honesty, non-violence and fidelity. Some behaviors are inherently better than others. Evil is evil, in that it celebrates the self at the expense of others.[7] Is this not a truth? And there is this: If there is a transcendent morality: Where does it come from? If there is "Truth:" What is its source? The atheist is hard pressed at this point to give a rational answer. In the world of the 'accidental cosmos', a world without purpose or meaning the notion of a transcendent morality is meaningless. And a notion of Evil and Good are merely the artificial constructs of human beings – legislating a societal code of morality according to their own interests or prejudices.

Take it then to religions: Can all religious belief really be of equal value? Some will argue that because of a some similar moral code they are at bottom, essentially the same. But the truth of the matter is exactly the opposite. The world's major religions are at odds on so very many essential points and only superficially similar. They disagree on the nature of who God is, on the nature of man, the existence and meaning of sin, on creation, and heaven and hell. Hinduism teaches evil is an illusion. Islam says that Allah could not have a son. Christianity teaches that the death and rising of the Son of God, Jesus, is essential for the salvation of Mankind. And the list goes on. These truths that they teach are mutually exclusive. Are we to embrace the religious beliefs of cannibals or Satanic cults that call for child sacrifice? And what of Muslim terrorists? Are their beliefs equally valid? As Geisler and Turek again point out: "Contrary to popular opinion, major world religions do not 'all teach the same things.' They have essential differences and only superficial agreements. All religions cannot be true, because they teach opposites."[8]

So I hope we've set the table. We've talked about world-views and the nature of "Truth" and briefly surveyed some competing systems of religious thought. But there is one very big and legitimate question that we've got to answer. How can God and evil coexist. So that's where were headed next.

CHAPTER 2
THE BIG QUESTION OF EVIL

Evil is all around us. There is suffering in every form and aspect of life. All creatures die. Most all die in pain. Man has the special privilege of recognizing his impermanence and living in the shadow of our own extinction. We exist in a world dominated, it would seem, by hate and crime and terror. Murder, rape, child abuse, unfaithfulness, cruelty and cupidity are our legacy. Our heritage has bequeathed us Joseph Stalin and Jeffrey Dahlmer, Columbine, the attack on the Twin Towers and the atrocities of ISIS We see starving children, and cancer wards, and an explosion of pedophilia. We face diseases that can rob us of control of our own bodies, or perhaps worse, diseases that may render us oblivious to our past, our surroundings, or our very selves. We are outraged. We are shaken to our very souls. Where is God in all of this? Thus the argument: This cannot be the work of a God of love. Surely this God cannot exist. If He does, either He is not all powerful or cannot be a God of love.

THE BIG QUESTION OF EVIL

Thus is the Big Question: How can a God that is all good, all powerful and all loving allow evil to exist? This is the most significant challenge – not just for Christianity – but for any world view – whether we believe in one God, many gods or none at all.

Consider the entailments of the question itself. Look at that very sense of outrage that we feel when confronted by evil. In that very emotion we are exercising judgment and we implicitly recognize the existence of a right standard of conduct. When we condemn the act or the evildoer, we tacitly acknowledge the reality of a Law in our hearts; the Law of Right and Wrong. So if someone uses the existence of evil to deny the existence of God, they destroy the standard on which to judge what is good and what is evil. Because without God; without a source for the Law of Right and Wrong: Everything becomes just preference. It becomes 'Just do what is useful' or 'Do what you prefer.' And yet we know evil when we see it. There is no escape from its reality. That reality, that ultimate standard is God.[9] [10] So in denying God on the basis of evil we deny the existence of evil itself.

You see a moral law assumes a source. If we are here by accident, the serendipitous result of the right biology, then there is no standard by which to judge. 'How can God condone such evil in the world?' The question becomes meaningless. No evolutionary process could ever explain the existence of a moral law. Without God, the existence of any moral standards could only be viewed as practical rules for the smooth running and perpetuation of society and the species. If we are but animals on what basis can we base a moral code? So we are left with utilitarianism, pure and simple. In the end it justifies anything. We have seen the workings of its cruel logic in the horrors all around us. The actions of the great icons of atheism and God-denial; Stalin, Hitler and Mao, give witness to the ultimate logic of that world-view. The slaughter perpetrated in the name of atheism was the predictable outcome of a philosophy that denies the existence of God and puts Man in that place. In contrast the crimes done in the 'name of the Christian religion' reflect the denial of Christ and his teachings.

To recognize that evil exists, and it does exist, is to recognize that there is a standard on which to judge right and wrong. The existence of the standard points to a source. That source is God. Christian apologist Dr. Ravi Zacharias states the case perfectly in his book, 'Jesus Among Other Gods'. He writes, "Not one proponent of evolutionary ethics has explained how an impersonal, amoral first cause through a non-moral process has produced a moral basis of life, while at the same time denying any objective moral basis for good and evil."[11] Without God everything is just personal preference. Objective morality lives only if God lives.

Now some may point to the Eastern religious notion of Dualism, which seems to have infiltrated so much of Western thought in the last several decades. [Recall when the Beatles went all Eastern with the Majrahah Mahesh Yogi back in the 60's.] Simply stated Dualism sees the universe as being controlled by the struggle between two independent divine beings or forces representing ultimate good and ultimate evil. The Chinese call this Yin and Yang, and see it as the battle on the one hand between the negative, dark and feminine and on the other hand the positive, bright and masculine. It is all part of the ultimate reality. It carries with it the notion that both evil and good are coequal parts of the transcendent reality present in all of us. The flaw in the theory again lies in the very fact of defining the concept of evil. Just that concept presumes a standard. No matter the 'personal beliefs' of Yin and Yang, both cannot be objectively good. C.S. Lewis writes in Mere Christianity, "Whatever the two powers think about it, and whatever we humans, at the moment happen to like, one of them is actually wrong, actually mistaken in regarding itself as good."[12] Even those who hold to this philosophy implicitly recognize this, that a standard exists, which one of powers fails to meet. Again that standard, that transcendent concept of good indicates a source above and beyond the Yin and the Yang. That source is God.

So let's get back to the meat of the question. Is it that God is perhaps not all powerful? Or perhaps He is not all good? What is the reason for the existence of evil in the universe?

Now perhaps you have noticed that inherent in this whole discussion of good and evil is the notion of free will. Nothing can be evil, no value can be attached to actions without this concept. So we are left with man as an agent with free will. And with this notion comes the ability to choose one's own course of action. In so doing we become a source for the evil in the world. We have seen that the standard does exist. Yet it is in the nature of man to try and set up a world in which he is independent of that standard. This is our rebellion. This is the story of the fall, both Man's and Satan's; the attempt to set up for ourselves, some sort of 'meaningful', existence outside of the transcendent moral standard. This is an existence without God.

We've seen that the logic of atheism renders 'evil' a meaningless term. And dualism and paganism, the idea that there are many less than all-powerful gods, again robs the term of meaning. Which god shall we choose to please? Which standard shall we pursue? Only the concept of God, as an all-powerful, loving creator, with the ultimate good inherent in His character, can explain the notion of evil in a logically coherent manner.

Now God could have created a world in which men and women would be able to sin. But that would not be a world without the highest ideal: Love. To have love we must be able to choose NOT to love. That involves free will. Without it there would be no meaningful relationships either between men and women or between God and His creation. God has made man capable of choosing the good….but also free to choose not to love; to choose evil.[13] Implicit in that choosing is the notion that our real-world choice will bring with it consequences, to both ourselves and our world.

The Scripture tells us that God is holy beyond comprehension, a righteous judge opposed to unjust and perfect and without blemish in His character. He is Love itself. So, if present in the nature and character of God, is all that is good, moral and just, then to know Him is the ultimate good. And evil can be defined as the choice we make to separate ourselves from Him when we reject Him. And we reject Him when we ignore his ways. It is all a matter of free will. Jesus speaks to this in Matthew. 22:37 *"Love the Lord your God with all your heart and with all your soul and with all your mind."* When Jesus gives the command to love, it pre-supposes the ability to refuse to do so. It is our choice. When Jesus gives this command too, it is a call to adhere to a life in the very center of His will, to become one with the very essence of life. The greatest good then would be to plug in to the power of the universe, to love the God who by his nature is all-good. To embrace that standard then would preclude the possibility of evil. To reject it is to open the door to its existence. Love is the ultimate good. One cannot even conceive of love as an involuntary response. It is only logical then that in order to experience this ultimate good of perfect love we must be free to reject that love, to renounce the ultimate good.[14]

This is the aspect of Christ's teaching that speaks to the very meaning of life. It is not our individual happiness, nor the ideal of achieving the greatest good for the greatest number that is the ultimate purpose of life. Meaning is found in the knowledge and love of God. Man's place in the Genesis story speaks of the relationship of both Adam and Eve to their Creator. The Bible tells us that they walked with God. And they walked with God by choice. When they rebelled, it was an act of free will. So we muse *choose* to love God. A loving personal relationship is possible only if we have the free will to accept or reject Him. In a universe where love is the highest virtue, the potential for evil will always be present. Yet since love is the highest value, and God is the essential expression of that value, because it resides there in His nature, then to choose love, to choose God, will provide the ultimate meaning in life. Our purpose then, is found in our relationship to Him. It is His will that we, as spiritual beings, freely choose to love and relate to Him. But love is only conceivable in a world in which we have the ability to reject love and chose evil. The conclusion: Fulfillment then is found in a knowledge of, and relationship with, God.[15] [16]

WORLD-VIEW IMPLICATIONS

The fact that 'Evil' cannot even be defined without a standard of the 'Good' or the way things ought to be, strikes a serious blow to two of the major world-views. No Materialist or Atheist explanation of the origin of the Universe - one that holds that the Cosmos just 'poofed' into existence out of nothing – has ever been able to explain a transcendent moral basis for life. In other words, it has been able to define neither the origin nor the nature of 'Good' and 'Evil.'

This same problem confronts both Dualism and Pantheism. In Dualism, the Yin and the Yang, the Light Force and the Dark Force, also lack a standard by which to define morality. And as to the Pantheist: One god's good is another god's evil.

In contrast, the Theistic World-view – (which includes Judaism, Christianity and Islam) - does offer an explanation for the existence of both 'Good' and 'Evil'.

The moral law comes from a Creator / Lawgiver. Goodness is inseperable from His character.

Evil comes through the operation of human free will. 'Good' and 'Evil' then are a product of human choice.

CHAPTER 3
ORIGINS

There are several basic world-views, or ways of looking at reality. These are Theism, Materialism, Deism and Pantheism. Each of these world-views – and their subsets, (such as Christianity and Islam being subsets of Theism) – must answer five essential questions: Origin, Identity, Meaning, Morality and Destiny. That's where Truth comes in. The various world-views are making claims about the Truth; trying to explain reality. Take Christianity for instance. It claims to interpret the world in a 'real' way. While faith may be necessary; it is not a blind faith that is required but one based on 'the way things are.' It provides an explanation of 'how the world works.' And each of these world-views – including scientific Materialism – must stand the tests of rationality, coherence and internal consistency. They all must be weighed against the evidence. And we'll see that as we unpack the science of the thing – that is precisely where 'scientific Materialism' will face its greatest challenge.

ORIGINS

"The heavens declare the glory of God; And the firmament shows His handiwork." (Psalm 19:1)

Atheism or Materialism has a real problem. You see the Atheist / Materialist point of view is this: Everything must be able to be explained by material causes. And that's where 'science' itself has seemed to throw up a major road block. We'll also find that what scientists now know about the origin of the Universe also poses major problems for Buddhists, Hindus, New Agers and others of the Pantheistic world-view. But for now we'll just concern ourselves with the Materialist point of view.] Another name for Materialism is Naturalism and it postulates that the laws of science are all we need to understand the universe. It holds that there is no first, or ultimate cause. There is no design apparent in nature, and therefore no purpose. The implications of this belief are enormous. If there is no purpose, if all of being is the result of accidental, impersonal forces, then there can be no evil, for there is no morality, for there is no source for such an ultimate morality. Oxford's Richard Dawkins puts it in startlingly candid terms. "There is at the bottom of it all no good, no evil, no purpose, nothing but blind pitiless indifference. DNA neither knows nor cares. DNA just is, and we dance to its music."[17]

The Materialist / Scientific way of knowing then sees the entire cosmos, including man himself, as the product of accidental forces. If man is an accident it must necessarily follow that life itself is meaningless. Meaning only exists as we define it. And in modernist thought only science is competent to reveal knowledge and define existence. Writing in the New York Review of Books in January 1997, noted apologist for naturalism, and Professor of Genetics at Harvard Richard Lewontin put the position most succinctly. "The problem is to get them to reject irrational and supernatural explanations of the world, the demons that exist only in their imaginations, and to accept …science as the only begetter of truth. We exist as material beings in a material world, all of whose phenomena are the consequences of material relations among material entities." Lewontin further admits in the same article that it is not the compelling nature of the evidence that leads to such a conclusion but a prior commitment to processes "that produce material explanations."[18]

And therein lies the rub. The scientific community has for the most part, established a philosophical theory which rules out anything but matter; attempting to explain the existence of matter by first ruling out any cause for matter.) Dr Philip Johnson writing in 'Is God Constitutional? (Part 2)', tackles this very question, "This is best seen in terms of the history of life, where it is axiomatic with evolutionary biologists and chemists that only purposeless, unintelligent material processes were involved in creating the immensely complex and diverse forms of life that exist today."[19]

As we go on to consider the science of the thing it is essential that we understand this: Materialism by definition excludes the consideration of outside forces. It can only follow then that a creative outside force, i.e. God, must by assumption be excluded. In effect it is saying; 'When we consider the origin of man and the cosmos we will only consider natural, material causes. Aha! We have found that man is the product of natural material causes alone.' The assumption that everything is the result of material processes alone is in place before the evidence is even considered.

But there's a slight problem with this 'scientific' view. It is actually opposed to the findings of modern science. So let's look at the Materialist World-view. Dr Stephen Meyer explains. In the beginning, in eternity past, there were Particles. Over time, Particles became complex living stuff. Over time, Living Stuff became aware. Then Living Stuff conceived of God. (This of course is directly opposed to the Theistic World-view which holds that God came first and then came Matter.) So the materialist offers us a Universe in which there is no design, no purpose and of course, no God. Uber-Atheist Richard Dawkins offers that the Cosmos came from undirected mindless processes. And intelligence came late to that party…..therefore there is no design – just Chance. So the Materialist view is that the Universe is: Eternal, Self-Existent, Self-Creating, Self-Organizing and Autonomous from Outside Forces.[20] And this was the view that was holding sway in the scientific community during the 19th and into the 20th century. Even Einstein believed in the eternal universe.

And then scientists began to suspect, then formulate a theory and finally develop several lines of evidence toward a new reality. The Universe had a beginning. They called that generating event: The Big Bang. And that realization changed everything.

It all really began during the second decade of the last century, brought to the forefront by a German scientist with unkempt hair by the name of Albert Einstein. He was working up his Theory of General Relativity and his conclusions were moving him toward a reality that he found personally very uncomfortable. His work with the equations of General Relativity meant "that space-time as whole must be warped and curved back on itself, which in itself would cause matter to move, shrinking uncontrollably under its own gravity. Thus, as early as 1917, Einstein and others realized that the equations of general relativity did not describe a static universe,"21 and that all time matter and space had to have a beginning. And that's not how he wanted things to be. Authors Geisler and Turek put it this way. "He wanted the universe to be self-existent – not reliant on any outside cause – but the universe appeared to be one giant effect. In fact, Einstein so disliked the implications of General Relativity – a theory that is now proven accurate to five decimal places – that he introduced a cosmological constant (which some have since called a 'fudge factor') into equations in order to show that the universe is static and to avoid an absolute beginning." This 'cosmological constant' was, on his part, a wishful theory that would maintain the fiction of a static universe with no beginning. But subsequent observations and experimentation didn't support that and Einstein would later own that notion of cosmological constant was "the biggest blunder of my life." Just a few years later, Arthur Eddington "conducted an experiment during a solar eclipse" that proved Einstein's Theory of Relativity – with one caveat however. The universe did indeed have a beginning. What's more, Willem de Sitter proved that General Relativity absolutely required an expanding Universe.[22]

Then in 1927. Edwin Hubble actually observed evidence for an expanding Universe from his newly built space telescope. This ran against the grain of centuries of scientific thought. As Luke Matin, author of the website Physics of the Universe writes: "Hubble started to notice that the light coming from these galaxies was shifted a little towards the red end of the spectrum due to the Doppler effect (known as 'redshift'), which indicated that the galaxies were moving away.... Hubble concluded that the galaxies and clusters of galaxies were in fact flying apart from each other at great speed, and that the universe was therefore definitively growing in size." And if the universe was moving apart it had to have had a begininng.[23] Geisler and Turek offer this picture. Think of it this way: If the universe is expanding then in your mind go back in time. Imagine the entire cosmos collapsing back on itself. It would eventually shrink to a point where it was "actually nothing. (ie no time, no space, no matter.) In other words, once there was nothing, and then BANG, there was something – the entire universe exploded into being."[24]

The implications of this were enormous. Just where did this first 'matter' come from? The First Law of Thermodynamics states that matter can be neither destroyed nor created. Yet it is just such a 'super-natural' event that is necessary to explain the spontaneous generation of hydrogen atoms out of the great nothing. A belief in pure materialism necessitates accepting that matter did generate itself out of nothing. This is a notion that runs contrary to the known laws of physics. More pointedly, it forces its atheistic adherents to claim as the basis for all existence that the universe was called into being out of nothing, by no one for no particular purpose and in violation of the physical laws generated by that act of creation.[25]

Think of it, for centuries scientific thought held to the theory of the eternal universe. The universe was always existent. If this model held true then there was no need to accept the idea of a Creator that formed the Cosmos. This idea was the atheist's greatest friend. The last 40 years or so though have seen one of the greatest shifts in scientific thought in history. Dr. Gerald Schroeder, a scholar in both physics and Biblical interpretation, sees the shift as representing "the most significant change science can ever make toward biblical philosophy."[26] The foundation for this change was laid in 1946 by Russian born scientist George Gamow, who proposed the Big Bang Theory. He held that the universe was the result of an intense concentration of energy. Gamow predicted that through the resultant explosion everything in the universe should be rushing away from each other with incredible speed. Work-a-day scientists Robert Wilson and Arno Penzias confirmed Gamow's theory in 1965 through the observation of background radiation. Later work has cemented the view among cosmologists that the universe must have had a starting point. Materialism requires that the causes go all the way back.....but now science itself was blowing up that pseudoscientific assumption. And not only was the universe expanding – and not only did it have a beginning – but it is huge beyond human comprehension. There are 100 billion stars – with at least 100 billion planets in our galaxy, the Milky Way alone. And that small to medium size galaxy is only one of 100 billion to 200 billion galaxies in the Cosmos.[27] The enormity of it all boggles the mind. Those believing in pure Materialism have been backed into a corner.

Consider the words of the agnostic astronomer Robert Jastrow from his book *God And The Astronomers*. "No explanation other than the Big Bang has been found for the fireball radiation. The clincher, which has convinced almost the last doubting Thomas, is that the radiation discovered by Penzias and Wilson has exactly the pattern of wavelengths expected for the light and heat produced in a great explosion. Supporters of the Steady State theory have tried desperately to find an alternative explanation, but they have failed. At the present time, the Big Bang theory has no competitors."[28] Later in his controversial book, Jastrow explained "NOW THREE LINES of evidence—the motions of the galaxies, the laws of thermodynamics, and the life story of the stars—pointed to one conclusion; all indicated that the Universe had a beginning." And that left old school scientists facing a very uncomfortable conclusion. "Consider the enormity of the problem. Science has proven that the Universe exploded into being at a certain moment. It asks, What cause produced this effect? Who or what put the matter and energy into the Universe? Was the Universe created out of nothing, or was it gathered together out of pre-existing materials? And science cannot answer these questions, because, according to the astronomers, in the first moments of its existence the Universe was compressed to an extraordinary degree, and consumed by the heat of a fire beyond human imagination. The shock of that instant must have destroyed every particle of evidence that could have yielded a clue to the cause of the great explosion…. For the scientist who has lived by his faith in the power of reason, the story ends like a bad dream. He has scaled the mountains of ignorance; he is about to conquer the highest peak; as he pulls himself over the final rock, he is greeted by a band of theologians who have been sitting there for centuries."[29]

CHAPTER 4
COSMIC FINE TUNING

Now the amazing thing about God is that….well, He's so amazing! You see, in the first two chapters we've let science establish the fact that the Universe had a beginning. And if a beginning…..well, then it had a Beginner. But there's so much more to the argument. God's purposes are revealed through the magnificent design of creation. We're going to look at just a little part of this; the cosmic fine tuning, if you will, that makes all of life possible. It's pretty neat stuff.

COSMIC FINE TUNING

We'll start by talking about the existence and fine-tuning of the universal constants. These constants need to be precisely what they are in order to have life exist here or anywhere in the entire cosmos. The degree of inter-related precision is almost unimaginable and flies in the face of all statistical probability. But to begin the discussion of this area we should perhaps consider the thought that according to the laws of relativity and cosmology, nothing at all should even exist. We know this because when matter is formed from energy in particle form, anti-matter is formed along with it - particle for particle. Though in their nature they are essentially the same, when they collide they annihilate each other. This then should have been a zero sum game. No matter should have survived. Sooo….there should be nothing at all; no Universe, no us. But for a reason still mysterious, one particle of matter in 10 billion survives when its anti-matter partner is destroyed. From this came all matter, all life. As Gerald Schroeder describes it in the Science of God, the formation of surviving matter "…took place in the first one hundred thousandth of a second following the big bang. We, or at least the building blocks from which we would be formed fifteen billion years later, were written into the universe at its earliest moments."[30]

[NOTE: Now, if you notice, and I'm sure you have, Dr Schroeder is operating under the assumption that the Universe is billions of years old. In discussing these matters we will allow each scientist to state his case in the terms that he believes apply. Dr Schroeder's position is somewhat unique. He is a biblical scholar and a former professor of physics at MIT. And if I'm understanding him correctly, he is both a believer in the six days of creation and a multi-billion year old universe. I'll let the good doctor try to explain it. Dr Schroeder believes there is no real conflict between a six-day creation and a Cosmos that is billions of years old. It all depends on the location from which one is measuring time. After all, it was Einstein who revolutionized our understanding of time and how it is relative, varying with the factors of velocity and gravity. Science author Scott Youngren explains. "Whoever inspired the Bible clearly understood both the relativity of time and the ratio at which Earth time converts to cosmic time…. Einstein demonstrated that time is relative, and the relativity of time has been subsequently tested and verified thousands of times." That's the set up for what Dr Schroeder has to say. "A common error in exploring the brief biblical age of the universe relative to the discoveries of cosmology is to view the universe from a specific location rather than choosing a reference frame that embraces the entire universe and retains that universal perspective for the entire six days. This cosmic clock records the passage of one minute while we on Earth experience a million million minutes. …At this million-million-to-one ratio those 120 million Earth years lasted a mere hour. That's the peer-reviewed physics and the biblical tradition of this discussion. Now for the modern theology: What does all this mean for the age of the universe? In terms of days and years and millennia, this stretching of the cosmic perception of time by a factor of a million million, the division of fifteen billion years by a million million reduces those fifteen billion years to six days!"[31]

I myself am no scientist – and at this time take no position on the matter other than I believe in the inerrancy of Scripture and truth of of the biblical account. But Gerald Schroeder believes he has found a way in which both are true. There are sincere and committed Christians on both sides of this debate. Some will be more 'creative' in attempting to reconcile the timeless Truth of the Biblical account with the current state of science. In the end, Scripture cannot be compromised. But in the process we will honor the perspective of the scientists we quote – not dismissing very solid arguments on the basis of a disagreement as to the chronology and methodology of the creation event.]

We return now the matter at hand. The amazing story of the universal constants continues to get even more amazing. What that story shows is that those universal constants, need to be just what they are in order for life to be even possible anywhere. And the more we understand the precision that is necessary and the overlapping dependence and delicate relationship between these variables the more we see the mark of unmistakable design. Here are some examples.

THE ELECTROMAGNETIC FORCE

The electromagnetic force is 10 to the 38th power stronger than the force of gravity. For one thing this regulates the rate at which stars burn. If the ratio were just a little larger it would result in massive stars burning too fast and unevenly to support life. If smaller it would render the formation of heavy elements impossible. But just the variation of the gravitational force constant alone would effect either the life chemistry or the formation of certain essential elements.

THE STRONG NUCLEAR FORCE

Then there is the strong nuclear force constant. If it were just a little larger it would mean no hydrogen would form and no life chemistry would be possible. If it were smaller then only hydrogen would form and again the chemistry of life would be absent.

THE WEAK NUCLEAR FORCE

Another example is the weak nuclear force constant. A variance in this factor would affect the levels of helium and hydrogen. The resulting imbalance again would affect the ability to produce heavy elements, and again be fatal to the processes of life chemistry.

ELECTRON TO PROTON MASS RATIO

Changes in the ratio of electron to proton mass critically influences chemical bonding.

EXPANSION RATE OF THE UNIVERSE

And there is the expansion rate of the universe. A more rapidly expanding cosmos would mean that galaxies would not have the chance to form. With slower expansion we would see, (or actually we wouldn't see), the universe collapse before the formation of stars.

The list goes on. Other factors critical to the ability to form life include the initial uniformity of radiation, the entropy level, the average distances between stars, and galaxies, and even the number of effective dimensions in the early universe making the coexistence of gravity, quantum mechanics and relativity impossible. And there is the energy present in the big bang. The precision required for the existence of life has been calculated at one part in 10 to the 120th power. Again the list goes on, but I won't. One source catalogs no less than 34 of these constants. The point is made. Precision is necessary not only in each of the individual factors, but also in their relationships to each other. It has been calculated that the chance of even one of them being what it is, is incredibly small. Like winning the lottery. To see the unbelievable coincidence of all of these constants coming together in such a precise way as to produce life, is like winning the lottery a billion times over. The hand of the Designer is showing. It takes an incredible amount of obstinacy to deny this evidence.[32] [33] [34]

Nobel laureate Arno Penzias weighs in with his conclusion. "Astronomy leads us to a unique event, a universe which was created out of nothing, one with the very delicate balance needed to provide exactly the conditions required to permit life, and one which has an underlying (one might say 'supernatural') plan."35 Alan Sandage adds this in a similar vein. "I find it quite improbable that such order came out of chaos. There has to be some organizing principle. God to me is a mystery but is the explanation for the miracle of existence, why there is something instead of nothing."[36]

And there is yet more evidence to unfold. Having looked at mathematical form and the incredible existence and relationship between the universal constants, we now go to a third area of evidence for the presence of design; the initial conditions critical for the formation of life on earth. Necessary to the existence of life is of course a stable environment for its development. Science has found that we not only live in a remarkably stable galaxy but a remarkably precise position within that galaxy. Only at a narrowly defined distance from the center of a galaxy can a star maintain its position within that galaxy, allowing the conditions of life to develop. That is just where our star, the sun is located. This means that we are in an area that is more secure than possibly anywhere else in the universe, safe from the disrupting influence of other stars.

However, position alone is not the only remarkable factor. The internal arrangement of our solar system seems to be quite unique. The very arrangement of planets within the Sun's system seems required to ensure its stability. And to many scientists, this lay-out makes unlikely the existence of another life-capable planet within any galaxy in our universe.[37] It begins with the very size of the sun. A smaller star would be incapable of supporting life. The earth's proximity to the Sun is another factor. We exist in what scientists have defined as the life zone. Gravitational interaction has greatly slowed our rotational period, eliminating the extremes in temperature that would other wise destroy all life.[38] Then there is the presence of Jupiter. Though its location has a profound destabilizing effect on especially the orbits of the inner planets, its existence is necessary to the stability of our system. Such a large planet has not been found so far out in any other known planetary system. Its presence protects us from comet showers that would be fatally disrupting to life on earth.

The specific arrangement of planetary bodies within the system is also responsible for the earth's uniquely circular orbit. Our climatic stability depends on this. Other factors influencing the climate are the axial tilt and the specific arrangement of the landmass. This allows for not only the progression of seasons but ensures that they are not too severe. The formation and presence of the moon is another contributing factor to this planet's ability to sustain life. Its formation through the collision of a small planet with the earth made possible the life-nurturing atmosphere that we have. This precise atmosphere enables water to be present in all three forms, a necessary condition for life. The gravitational pull of the moon also slows the surface winds which otherwise would have velocities of over 500 mph. Yet another remarkable factor is the existence of the Van Allen radiation field. This magnetic field, produced by our nickel core, protects the planet from radiation bombardment. Within our solar system only Mercury has a magnetic field and that at a level much too small to be of much protective value. These are just a few examples of the unique arrangements from which we benefit so much. Our solar system seems uniquely designed to make possible our existence.[39]

In fact it all seems like a big set up job. It is the study of intelligent design that has given us a rational, scientific approach to understanding the ramifications of understanding that. It shows us the patterns of design inherent in every level of nature; from sub-atomic to micro-biotic, from DNA to the arrangement of the cosmos. Reviewing the evidence, astronomer George Greenstein offers this. "As we survey all the evidence, the thought insistently arises that some supernatural agency - or, rather, Agency - must be involved. Is it possible that suddenly, without intending to, we have stumbled upon scientific proof of the existence of a Supreme Being? Was it God who stepped in and so providentially crafted the cosmos for our benefit?"[40]

WORLD-VIEW IMPLICATIONS

Now the Humanist Manifesto, and the tenets of materialism may declare that matter is self existent and not created, but the clear evidence of intelligent design declares them wrong. Pure materialism is fraught with problems. Its most basic being the fact that it requires the violation of both the first and second laws of thermodynamics. Science is now in agreement with the first words of the Bible, "*In the beginning…*". The Big Bang says there was a beginning. Yet materialism claims that matter is self-existent. There is a problem in that. For matter to come into being without cause from the great nothing violates the law of thermodynamics.[41] For matter to have had a beginning however requires a cause. For the organization of matter into the many interdependent highly designed patterns that characterize creation from this completely uncaused beginning violates the Second Law of Thermodynamics. It tells us we should witness a cosmos of increasing disorder. Instead we find the opposite, clear evidence for the presence of an intelligent agent behind the wonderful workings of the world we know. But if materialism has failed us, where do we search for truth? So, we'll close this chapter with the words of Frank Tipler, Professor of Mathematical Physics who went from God-denier to committed Christian during his 'Truth Journey'. "When I began my career as a cosmologist some twenty years ago, I was a convinced atheist. I never in my wildest dreams imagined that one day I would be writing a book purporting to show that the central claims of Judeo-Christian theology are in fact true, that these claims are straightforward deductions of the laws of physics as we now understand them. I have been forced into these conclusions by the inexorable logic of my own special branch of physics."[42] It's the science that is moving astronomers and cosmologists toward acceptance of the truth claims of Scripture. God is a God of order and design. As the psalmist noted: *"The heavens proclaim the glory of God. The skies display his craftsmanship. Day after day they continue to speak; night after night they make him known."* (Psalm 19:1-2) (NLT)

CHAPTER 5
THE PROBLEM OF LIFE

Now as we've been unpacking the evidence surrounding the Creation Event and the amazing design of the Cosmos, we can note that the evidence so far has not been kind to the Materialist cause. A Universe with a beginning builds the argument for an Intelligent Source outside of time and space that somehow caused time and space and energy to come into being. There is the little matter of the fine tuning of the cosmic constants. That life can exist at all seems a miracle. Even in this amazingly vast and expanding universe the odds against it are astronomical. And that's what we'll tackle next - the issue of 'Life' itself.

THE PROBLEM OF 'LIFE'

The Materialist / Atheists have a real problem to solve. They must explain the origin of life. And that often leads to them reasoning against the evidence. Richard Lewontin is a Harvard geneticist who DOES NOT believe in a Grand Designer. He wants us all to be perfectly clear about that. But Dr Lewontin once wrote that organisms "appear to have been carefully and artfully designed." Later Lewontin goes on to explain that the "'perfection of organisms' is often illusory."43 So we mustn't look to the evidence to draw our conclusions. But in another, perhaps more honest setting, Richard Lewontin gives us this. "Our willingness to accept scientific claims that are against common sense is the key to an understanding of the real struggle between science and the supernatural. We take the side of science in spite of the patent absurdity of some of its constructs.... It is not that the methods and institutions of science somehow compel us to accept a material explanation of the phenomenal world, but, on the contrary, that we are forced by our a priori adherence to material causes to create an apparatus of investigation and a set of concepts that produce material explanations, no matter how counter-intuitive, no matter how mystifying to the uninitiated. Moreover, that materialism is absolute, for we cannot allow a Divine Foot in the door."[44] The only explanation allowed past the doors of Academy is Materialism. That is true even when it flies in the face of the evidence. Thus is the wisdom of 'objective science'.

'Life' has 7 basic characteristics. It is composed of cells, has different levels of organization, uses energy, responds to its environment, grows, reproduces and adapts to its surroundings.45 One of the requirements of life is that it has proteins, or strings of amino acids. Now where could that possibly come from? What many Materialists advance is a theory of the chemical evolution of life. There was this 'primordial soup' and then stuff happened and like magic, life came into being. This is called Abiogenesis, "the theory that under the proper conditions life can arise spontaneously from non-living molecules." Russian scientist Alexandr Ivanovich Oparin advanced this theory, widely accepted by many Darwinists. Jerry Bergman of Creation.com explains. "Oparin 'postulated that life may have evolved solely through random processes' in what he termed a biochemical 'soup' that he believed once existed in the oceans. The theory held that life evolved when organic molecules that originally rained into the primitive oceans from the atmosphere were energized by forces such as lightning, ultraviolet light, meteorites, deep-sea hydrothermal vents, hot springs, volcanoes, earthquakes, or electric discharges from the sun. If only the correct mix of chemicals and energy were present, life would be produced spontaneously. Almost a half century of research and millions of dollars have been expended to prove this idea—so far with few positive results and much negative evidence."[46] Evidence for the theory was hard to find. Then in 1953 came the Miller-Urey experiment which claimed to have created the first steps toward life in a test tube. Miller and Urey enclosed methane, ammonia, hydrogen and water vapor in sealed glass, boiled the soup and zapped it with 60.000 volts of electricity. The recipe was altered and over time some very small amounts of "biologically useful amino acids were formed."

But the longer term results were less favorable for the Abiogenesis crowd. Here's Bergman. "It was believed that the results were significant because some of the organic compounds produced were the building blocks of much more complex life units called proteins—the basic structure of all life. Although widely heralded by the press as 'proving' that life could have originated on the early earth under natural conditions (i.e. without intelligence), we now realize the experiment actually provided compelling evidence for exactly the opposite conclusion. For example, without all 20 amino acids as a set, most known protein types cannot be produced, and this critical step in abiogenesis could never have occurred." In addition the characteristics needed to produce amino acids useful for the productions of proteins were of the wrong type.[47] MIT scientist Seth Lloyd concluded that the chance of getting even "one small protein of 150 amino acids" from this type of action would be 1 in 1040,000.48 Another researcher found that the chances of assembling even one simple bacteria would be 1 in 1010,000,000,000. Information theorist Herbert Yockey of UC Berkley concluded: "The origin of life by chance in a primeval soup is impossible in probability in the same way that a perpetual motion machine is in probability."[49] And Chris Wills, a Professor of Biology and the University of California wisely concludes: "The biggest gap in evolutionary theory remains the origin of life itself… the gap between such a collection of molecules [amino acids and RNA] and even the most primitive cell remains enormous."[50]

The Problem of DNA

If the origin of life is a problem for atheists and materialists, the existence and nature of DNA is another. The mapping of the genome and related research that advanced our understanding of the nature of DNA has complicated the matter significantly. The issue is this: DNA is an actual language and language requires intelligence. Though not at all intending to make an argument for Intelligent Design, Bill Gates himself admitted as much when he said: "Human DNA is like a computer program but far, far more advanced than any software ever created."[51] DNA is made up of chemicals represented by the letters A, T, G, and C which provide instructions for the cell's make-up and actions through the way in which they are arranged. This is no simple language. Within every cell in our bodies are instructions that are 3 billion letters long. Like Bill Gates, the Director of the Human Genome Project, Dr Francis Collins, believes that we should "think of DNA as an instructional script, a software program, sitting in the nucleus of the cell."[52] Science writer Mario Seigle fleshes it out for us. "For it to be rightly called a language, it must contain the following elements: an alphabet or coding system, correct spelling, grammar (a proper arrangement of the words), meaning (semantics) and an intended purpose. Scientists have found the genetic code has all of these key elements[53]." Human language is the only other code ever found to have these characteristics. This does not exist elsewhere in nature; not in the bellowing of whales, the chattering of dolphins or the barking of dogs. And the origin of human language has always come from an intelligent source – human beings. Information specialist Perry Marshall explains the significance of this fact. "There has never existed a computer program that wasn't designed...[Whether it is] a code, or a program, or a message given through a language, there is always an intelligent mind behind it."[54] [55] So DNA then is the medium of information, the carrier if you will of this independent genetic information. And highly complex information of this order comes only from intelligent sources. As Lee Strobel points out in The Case for a Creator: The information carried by the DNA is responsible for "the building of biological machines that far outstrip human technological capabilities."[56]

Now the amount of information held by DNA is just incredible. Harvard researchers studying the use of DNA for information storage have managed to store 700 terabytes of information into a single gram of DNA.[57] In a non-computer setting, the info contained in a human DNA has been compared to that found in 384 volumes of the Encyclopedia Britannica. This is no simple code. Molecular biologist and author of *Evolution: A Theory in Crisis*, Michael Denton, lays it out for us. The genetic information found in each cell contains "artificial languages and their decoding systems, memory banks for information storage and retrieval, elegant control systems regulating the automated assembly of parts and components, error fail-safe and proof-reading devices utilized for quality control, assembly processes involving the principle of prefabrication and modular construction . . . [and a] capacity not equaled in any of our most advanced machines, for it would be capable of replicating its entire structure within a matter of a few hours."[58] There is no way that this vast and complex information could have evolved according to the proposed Darwinian mechanism. Professor of Information Systems, Werner Gitt sums it up. "The basic flaw of all evolutionary views is the origin of the information in living beings. It has never been shown that a coding system and semantic information could originate by itself [through matter] . . . The information theorems predict that this will never be possible. A purely material origin of life is thus [ruled out]"[59]

It was this sort of information that convinced the very famous committed atheist, Anthony Flew to change his tune a bit. While making it clear that he did not accept the Biblical version of God; when faced with the DNA evidence he said this: "Super-intelligence is the only good explanation for the origin of life and the complexity of nature."60 There are others in the scientific community that are beginning to see the light. Lee Strobel quotes biology professor Dean Kenyon who has reversed his former position as a believer in Darwinian evolution. Looking at the amount and complexity of information found in DNA he said: "This new realm of molecular genetics (is) where we see the most compelling evidence of design on the Earth."[61] [62]

Still there are many Materialists who deny even the possibly of a Divine Designer and insist that evolution must be the way in which these systems all came to be. Yet the evidence is increasingly against them. There are an increasing number within the scientific community ready to answer them. Arthur L Schawlow, winner of the 1981 Nobel Prize in Physics puts it this way. "It seems to me that when confronted with the marvels of life and the universe, one must ask why and not just how. The only possible answers are religious. . . . I find a need for God in the universe and in my own life."[63]

Yet many persist in unbelief despite the evidence. Among these there is a commitment to credit only material causes for the origin and existence of everything – even while current scientific belief in the Big Bang speaks of a time before matter & energy & time & the laws of physics – and therefore material causes ever existed. A Universe with a beginning – which the Big Bang posits – begs a beginning outside of materialism. Scripture puts it thusly: *"For the wrath of God is revealed from heaven against all ungodliness and unrighteousness of men, who suppress the truth in unrighteousness, because what may be known of God is manifest in them, for God has shown it to them. For since the creation of the world His invisible attributes are clearly seen, being understood by the things that are made, even His eternal power and Godhead, so that they are without excuse, because, although they knew God, they did not glorify Him as God, nor were thankful, but became futile in their thoughts, and their foolish hearts were darkened. Professing to be wise, they became fools."* (Romans 1:18- 22) And fools continue to "kick against the goads."

**** ****

In trying to explain the origin of life without reference to a Creator, the materialist faces many problems. Now we turn our attention to one of the cornerstones of atheistic thought: Evolution. It is the Holy Grail of anti-God materialists. Evolution remains a sacred article of faith among its initiates – despite the growing evidence against it. As we examine this issue we'll find that the Emperor has few if any clothes. Lucy's got a lot o' 'splainin' to do.

The Problems With Evolution

"Then God said, 'Let the earth bring forth the living creature according to its kind: cattle and creeping thing and beast of the earth, each according to its kind'; and it was so." (Genesis 1:24)

Whatever Robert Locke might be he wants to make one thing perfectly clear: He does not buy into the literal Creation story promulgated in the Bible. Here then is the beginning of an article he wrote titled: The Scientific Case Against Evolution, which was published in 2001. "*I AM NOT A CREATIONIST, and must confess that until recently, I treated people who questioned evolution with polite dismissal. But there has recently emerged a major trend in biology that has been suppressed in the mainstream media: evolution is in trouble. More importantly, this has absolutely nothing to do with religion but is due to the fact that the ongoing growth of biological knowledge keeps producing facts that contradict rather than confirm evolution.*"[64] So we'll agree with Mr Locke and use that as a jumping off point to present a cursory summary of just a few of the problems with Neo-Darwinian Evolutionary theory.

Evolutionary Theory Can't Explain the Origin of Life

This is the 'Really Big Argument.'

There is no plausible theory of how life grew out of chemical soup. No matter how many billions of years you propose the chance remains essentially zero. As Geisler & Turek point out in their book I Don't Have Enough Faith to Be an Atheist: Darwinists "don't even have an explanation for the source of non-living chemicals, much less an explanation for life."65

The Problem of DNA

Casey Luskin points to the inability of scientists to explain exactly where the massive amount of information contained in DNA may have come from. Science has been unable to explain the "high levels of complex and specified information" found in the genetic code.[66]

Limits to Evolutionary Change: Micro-evolution Yes! Macro-evolution No!

- According to evolutionary theory, mutations cause new information to enter the gene pool. Advantageous mutations then are reinforced by the mechanism of natural selection or the survival of the fittest. The surviving organisms will display the new characteristics dictated by the mutation and eventually, over countless generations, new organisms are formed. As Charles Darwin famously observed on the Galapagos Islands, the finches he saw there had beaks that adapted to the changing climatic conditions. Dry weather increased the population of finches with large beaks. It was easier to breakdown the hard seeds produced by that climate, (seeds being an essential *par*t of their diet). In wetter weather, small-beaked finches increased. But that wasn't macro-evolution. The changes were always cyclical. And the information that dictated beak size was already in the gene pool. You see, there are strict limits to change. Dogs remain dogs and finches keep on being finches. A couple of famous experiments have added to our understanding in this area. Scientists have conducted an experiment with fruit flies over hundreds of generations conducted over the course of three-and-one-half decades. "Instead of waiting for natural selection, researchers forced selection on hundreds of generations of fruit flies." Yet they found that: "There were many mutations, but none caught on, and the experiment ran into the limits of variation."67 Researchers concluded that: "Despite decades of sustained selection in relatively small, sexually reproducing laboratory populations, selection did not lead to the fixation of newly arising unconditionally advantageous alleles."[68] Fruit flies remained fruit flies.

Then there is the famous experiment begun by Dr Richard Lenski in 1988. It has followed the genetic development of over 60,000 generations of bacterium. But the observed changes produced only "disruption, degradation, or loss of genetic information.... Mutations that result in a gain of novel information have not been observed."69 As Geisler and Turek summarized it: "The surviving bacteria always stay bacteria. They do not evolve into another type of organism. That would be macro-evolution. Natural selection has never been observed to create new types."[70]

The Problem of Irreducible Complexity

Charles Darwin wrote in The Origin of Species: "If it could be demonstrated that any complex organ existed, which could not possibly have been formed by numerous, successive, slight modifications, my theory would absolutely break down. But I can find no such case."[71] Well, unfortunately for his theory, those complex organs have been found. In his book *Darwin's Black Box*, Michael Behe defines Irreducible Complexity as "A single system composed of several well-matched, interacting parts that contribute to the basic function, wherein the removal of any one of the parts causes the system to effectively cease functioning. An irreducibly complex system cannot be produced directly (that is, by continuously improving the initial function, which continues to work by the same mechanism) by slight, successive modifications of a precursor system, because any precursor to an irreducibly complex system that is missing a part is by definition nonfunctional."[72] Robert Locke simplifies it for us. Evolution cannot explain "how anything could evolve that doesn't make biological sense when incomplete. The wings of birds are the classic example: what good is half of one?"[73]

The more pressing problem for evolutionary theory is coming up with a mechanism that would get around this problem. Of what benefit to the organism is an eye that cannot yet see, or wings that cannot produce flight. How or why would an insentient nature choose for such as these?[74] According to the law of natural selection, nature could only select for components that in themselves produced a definite survival advantage for the organism. A sightless eye or flightless wings would produce no such advantage. In fact, "nature would select against the continued production of the miscellaneous parts if they are not producing immediate benefits to the organism." So how could the complex systems known to exist on all levels, from the molecular to the fully articulated organ systems ever be developed? Michael Behe in Darwin's Black Box argues exhaustively that it could not. Behe shows that on the molecular level, the information required by the complexity of the process requires more than a mere chemical reaction. Complex information screams design.[75] It is in Behe's phrase, "irreducibly complex." This describes a system that has several interacting components, the removal of any one of which would result in its failure. Behe uses the example of an everyday mousetrap. Remove a part and it is useless. Not any single part would catch any mice. It is the whole system that is necessary to make the system operable. In the natural, a system would have to be chosen in the whole. It could not logically be the result of countless, successive, minuscule modifications. It could not be the result of the Darwinian mechanism. Yet in nature so many of these systems do exist. Eyes and wings are but two examples. Each would have had to come into being as a unit.[76] This blows the theory of natural selection out of the water. Natural selection holds that each change must be useful. Each biological selection must give a survival advantage to the organism or it would not be selected. Behe argues convincingly in his thesis that so much of the cell life on the molecular level is in fact - irreducibly complex.[77]

All of these complex organs and functions would "require irreducibly complex systems that could not have developed in the gradual Darwinian fashion….Because the intermediaries would be nonfunctional," and therefore not survive. As Geisler & Turek conclude: "Irreducible complexity means that new life cannot come into existence by the Darwinian method of slight, successive changes over a long period of time."[78]

Transitional Forms Cannot Survive

– Darwinists propose that reptiles became birds. But how would the transitional forms be able to function? A partially developed system of wings or feathers would not provide an evolutionary advantage. And further, no viable mechanism for that change has been proposed.[79]

A Great Big Hole in the Fossil Record

Back in 1859 when Darwin first proposed his theory, he believed that fossil evidence collected in the ensuing years would fill the evidential gaps in his hypothesis. Unfortunately for Darwin the years have not served his theory well. As more and more fossils are gathered, it is becoming apparent that the intermediate forms just do not exist. Despite the ample and well organized record of fossil evidence available at this time there does not exist any evidence for either the traditional gradual theory of macro-evolution or the idea that 'progress' came in spurts. There are no forms that show that the basic body plans found during the Cambrian Explosion have altered or that new phyla have been built from earlier ones. Instead what the fossils do show is an existence throughout Earth's history. When new species have been formed the change has come quickly. This flies in the face of a Darwinian theory that calls for gradual change with many intermediate forms, all progressing up the ladder of complexity.

But this is just not the case. In numerous studies, whether concerning marine life or mammals, or mollusks no gradualism has been found. To the contrary, changes have been abrupt and have lacked the transitional forms linking organisms together. This can be seen most pointedly when studying the Cambrian Explosion, a period of time during which every major anatomical design seems to have appeared 'simultaneously.'[80] The evidence is world-wide. Fossils have been found from Canada to Africa to China. Fully developed organs, jointed appendages, lungs and eyes all come upon the scene at once. The change from single celled simplicity to multi-celled complexity was abrupt.[81] Further, the various phyla making their appearance during the Cambrian period are unique to that time. For the overwhelming majority of the Cambrian animals no ancestry can be traced. There is no record of their gradual appearance. This phenomenon is an "expression of design" in that it assembled animal life into the 50 known phyla. Thirty-seven of these survive to this day. Significantly not one has been added. There is no evidence for the evolutionary mechanism to have worked since that time. It remains a great mystery why the subsequent changes in animal life have all been contained within the various phyla. And in the millions of fossil specimens existing today there has been found no transitional form. I cannot stress this enough. The 'missing links' are still missing.[82] [83]

There Is NO Evolutionary Tree of Life

Computer analysis of the data has confirmed these conclusions. The computer models do not produce the neat 'tree of life' models long proposed in evolutionary circles. Analysis of the numerically encoded data solving for grouping animal life by the similarities and differences found, produces groupings that do not fit the evolutionary tree. Robert Locke, writing in an article for Front Page Magazine states, "When the computer is constrained to push the data into an evolutionary tree, it tends to generate trees with all species as individual twigs and no species forming the crucial lower branches of the tree that evolution demands." Locke points out that the former characterization of evolutionary relationships between animals, are somewhat arbitrary at best. Concentrating on one set of animal characteristics may produce one set of relationships, while looking at another may make those same relationships seem entirely illogical. This is further confirmed by analyzing the thousands of proteins that make up living organisms. Examining life on this basic level shows the same distinctness among species, as do the computer models that organize life by anatomical characteristics.[84] There is no clear pattern of descent.

So let's review some of the problems with the theory of Darwinian evolution. It rests on the notion that all life forms existent today are the result of infinitesimal changes across thousands of generations, as each adapted to the environmental conditions it was facing. The problem is, the fossil record does not support this. Instead it shows an explosion of life forms in the Cambrian period emerging complete and remaining unchanged.[85] Intelligent design proponent, William Dembski, summarizes the critique of Darwinism presented by Michael Denton in his book Evolution; A Theory in Crisis. The theory's weakness are many he points out. They include "...the origin of life, the origin of the genetic code, the origin of multi-cellular life, the origin of sexuality, the gaps in the fossil record, the biological big bang that occurred in the Cambrian era, the development of complex organ systems, and the development of irreducibly complex molecular machines."[86] It is precisely the most basic contentions of the evolutionary model that are the most weakly supported. Darwinian Theory has not been able to explain how amino acids became DNA, or find the link between reptile and bird or the early primates and man. And as more and more fossil evidence is assembled the problem of the 'missing link', the connecting transitional form - is increasingly evident. It is not just the link between ape and man that is missing, but the problem is evident across all times and species. Denton, an agnostic, writes this: "The infinitude of connecting links has still not been discovered and the fossil record is about as discontinuous as it was when Darwin was writing the Origin."[87] Scientists are increasingly questioning the fact that amino acids somehow altered themselves into DNA. The notion that this complex information appeared spontaneously out of nowhere and for no good reason is increasingly seen as an illogical idea, fit into a pre-existing theory. They are beginning to realize that the link between ape and human may be based more on conjecture fed by a theoretical prejudice than any solid scientific evidence.

Here's a final summation. First, there exists no documentary evidence for macro-evolution. Both biology and the fossil record show this is true. Secondly, the predicted transitional forms are absent. While there is evidence of new species having appeared, there are no linking forms above the family level. Next we must consider the incredible complexity of the DNA. Its storage capacity is several trillion times that of our most advanced computers. This suggests design. Science tells us that complex design can only be produced by an intelligent designer. Fourthly, evolution faces the problem of explaining the generation of life from non-living matter. The biochemistry is impossible. No linking form has been found between complex molecules and the simplest one celled life form. In fact science cannot conceive of an event of inanimate matter that can form even the most basic form of life. Lastly, the tenets of naturalism violate the first two laws of thermodynamics. The first states that in a closed system, matter can be neither created nor destroyed. The corollary of the second law is that any change in form is accompanied by a decrease in complexity. The increasing complexity then, required by evolutionary theory contradicts the known laws of science. The appearance of ever more complex forms would require an intelligent agent. A Creator, perhaps![88] [89] [90]

WORLD-VIEW IMPLICATIONS

So let's look at what we've discovered thus far. We've learned that every world-view; whether Biblical, Islamic, Eastern-Religious or Atheistic – must answer some very basic questions in order to prove valid. These are: origin, identity, meaning, morality and destiny. Of course these are all interrelated. Wrapped up in the answers is the most essential question of the existence and nature of God. The self-existent, eternal and all-powerful nature of a Theistic God will yield a different set of answers than the Pan-Theistic view which sees God as an irrational Force – or Materialism which posits that no God exists – and a world defined by the accidental interplay of cosmic forces. The answers we give will of course have its effect on how we view Truth and Morality. In a purely material world no objective morality can exist. It is all of our own construction. This was the preferred view of science for several centuries. But the foundation of that point of view began to crumble at the beginning of the 20th century as we discovered the scientific basis for the origin of the cosmos. You see the Atheist / Materialist point of view is this: Everything must be able to be explained by material causes. That's where 'science' itself has seemed to throw up a major road block.

As scientists like Hubble and Einstein and Jastrow began to uncover the evidence for a Universe with a definite beginning – (it came to be called the Big Bang) – the theory of a 'Cosmos that always was' crumbled. The Universe had a beginning – and therefore required a Beginner. We quoted Nobel Prize winner Arno Penzias. "Astronomy leads us to a unique event, a universe which was created out of nothing, one with the very delicate balance needed to provide exactly the conditions required to permit life, and one which has an underlying (one might say 'supernatural') plan."[91]

That discovery undermined not only the pre-existing architecture of scientific belief but also dealt a serious if not fatal blow to both Pantheism and Dualism, which rely upon the notion of an eternally-existing cosmos.

The precision and structure found in nature provides another strong argument for the existence of a Designer. There are the over 100 identified cosmological constants which must be precisely defined in order for life to exist at all. These include such forces as Electromagnetic Force, Strong Nuclear Force, Weak Nuclear Force and Expansion Rate of the Universe. Then we took on that centerpiece of Materialist thinking; Darwinian Evolution. We saw how evolution cannot explain the origin of life, nor the complexity of DNA. It can't get past the observable limits to evolutionary change. It falls flat when it comes up against irreducible complexity. As Robert Locke put it: Evolution cannot explain "how anything could evolve that doesn't make biological sense when incomplete. The wings of birds are the classic example: what good is half of one?"[92] Neither can it get past the great big holes in the fossil record that has not produced the intermediate forms predicted by the Darwinian theory of evolution. The case for a Creator / Designer is getting stronger!

PART II
SCRIPTURE ON TRIAL

CHAPTER 6
TESTING THE BIBLE

Up until now we've been making the case for a personal God. But the evidence we've looked at so far doesn't quite define who He is. At this point in the trial He could be either the God of the Bible or the Koran Who is very involved in ongoing operation of the Universe…….or at least the Deistic notion of a Creator God Who set the whole thing up and then went hands off. So to settle that Theism / Deism question – and start to draw some distinctions between the Islamic and Biblical views of reality, we'll spend our next segments looking at the Bible. Is it true? Is there evidence that it is what it claims; the very Word of God?

TESTING THE BIBLE

What is the Bible? Critics tell us it is nothing more than ancient mythology, with a sometimes confusing moral message mixed in. It is not based so much on historical fact as on the wishful folk tales of a much abused and abusing, ancient people. It is perhaps a record of that peoples' struggle to find meaning and purpose, but otherwise holds little value today. It is certainly of no more value than any of the other ancient 'sacred writings', such as the Koran or the Hindu Bhagavad-Gita. It is subjective. It is contradictory. It is a fairy tale.

When you examine the evidence however, you find it is nothing of the sort. It was a book written over the span of 1100 BC to approximately 100 AD by about 40 different authors. Somehow, throughout all that, it maintains a unity of theme and a consistency of purpose. It is a specific book. It names, names and places that while they may have originally been questioned, have time and again, without fail, been proven true by the investigations of ancient historians and archaeologists. The inquiries of science have not proven it wrong. In fact, as more becomes known, the accuracy of the limited Biblical pronouncements on the workings of the natural world have been confirmed. The Bible is a prophetic book. Its specificity and precision, means that its prophecies can be, and have been tested. The Bible has that record of fulfilled prophecy on which to stand. That fulfillment has been recorded in the more recently authored books of Scripture and by history itself. The more one examines the writings, meaning and record of the Bible, the more one must come to the conclusion that the Bible is one extraordinary book.

Now the Bible claims for itself the authority of being the very word of God. To a believer in pure naturalism this would seem a preposterous claim. But Scripture itself has held this consistently. If in the Old Testament we read 'The word of the Lord came to me', we see the Scriptural claim of this in action. The writers of the New Testament not only confirm this view of the Old Testament writings but claim scriptural authority for themselves. Whether on matters of prophecy or doctrine, the pronouncements found in the Bible are equivalent to the 'Word of God'. It is not that God gave the authors of these books the exact words necessarily, except in very rare instances perhaps. Rather it is the Spirit of God that has inspired their writings.

So we see a proliferation of styles among the many authors. Yet still the theme remains the same. It is this conception of the Bible as the word of God that has naturally led Christian theologians to the conclusion that scripture must necessarily be inerrant. The in-errancy of scripture means that Gods words were accurately expressed in the original writings. This does not require a literal reading of the whole document. The Bible must be interpreted in the same sense that the authors intended. There is throughout the whole the use of poetry, metaphors and the various figures of speech. In the opening passages of Genesis, describing the creation, we see an accurate rendering of events, though without the detail that might be expected or wished by some today.

We must also remember that various natural phenomena are described the way they appear rather than in some scientifically accurate way. One example would be the use of the terms sunrise and sunset. We know today of course that it is not the Sun that is moving at all, but the rotation of the earth that causes the phenomena we are describing. Yet we continue to use those terms to this day. How much more this must have been true in a less scientifically sophisticated age. None of these techniques makes the passages any less accurate for the author's purposes. For example, the Song of Solomon is a poem. Chronicles I & II are historical records. Their different literary natures make neither more nor less true.[93] Admittedly though the in-errancy of scripture can only be tested by its' accuracy. Let's see how its accuracy holds up against the evidence.

Testing the Scriptures

We'll begin to test the veracity of the Scriptures by looking at the documents themselves. How do we know that what we are reading is the 'Word of God'? Almost unanimously the early church accepted the Old Testament scriptures of the Judaic tradition. As to the New Testament, the 27 Books were finally officially established by the ratification of Church Councils held during the 4th century. Both the Eastern and Western forms of the Church adopted the books now widely held as being worthy of the designation of Holy Scripture. This was in many ways an approval of the already held practices of the Church at large. It must be understood that this was not imposed from on high. This was instead a clarifying process.

Through the first few centuries of the new faith, the various centers of the Church had gone through a process of testing the possible choices of New Testament literature. The books that survived this process are those that were best suited to the purpose.

They are those that best reflected the true nature of Christ's teaching. Many works were accepted, first, by the Church-at-large, and finally by the formal councils of the faith. There were several other 'Gospels' that were rejected. But it was not a result of some internal political struggle or attempt to hide some 'truth' that would in some way compromise the power or position of the Church. The books that made it into the canon did so because of the internal witness of the Holy Spirit, reflected by adherence to 3 specific criteria. These included; first the direct authorship or sanction of an Apostle, secondly wide recognition and usage by the churches, and finally a test of its content. Did that particular work reflect the standards and teachings of the Christian message?

The Gospels of Matthew, Mark, Luke and John were found to have met these tests. For many reasons, many of the 'gospels' extant at the time did not. These were to begin with, later works, written between the 2nd and 5th centuries, and it therefore follows that they had no connection with an Apostle. [Even liberal scholarship admits that the canon of the Bible was complete by the end of the first century – and most serious researchers believe it was penned before the destruction of Jerusalem in AD 70; just thirty-some years after Christ's death and resurrection.] Perhaps the most famous of these is the Gospel of Thomas. Even a quick read of just some of its verses reveals a fatal variance with the norms of Christian teaching. Thomas is a gospel of an almost eastern philosophy, with a marked pantheistic theme. God is found in the very matter of creation. This is in no way a Christian idea, and the Church-at-large and in council recognized this. In addition there is an inferiority of women inherent in its teachings. So when these other books were rejected, it was because they did not 'jive' with the teachings of Jesus. They did not conform to the Christian understanding of the world.[94] [95]

In addition we can be more than reasonably certain that the Bible we read today is, in all of its essentials, and over 99% of its details an accurate representation of the original work. By the standard objective tests applied by historians, the New Testament is by far the most reliable of any ancient historical writing. There are over 5000 copies just in the original Greek, over 24,600 copies or fragments of copies overall. More than 1700 copies of the Old Testament in Hebrew are in existence. Homer's Iliad is the next most documented work, with about 640 copies. Only 10 copies of Julius Caesar's Gallic Wars can be found. The accuracy of these ancient secular works is never questioned. Furthermore the gap between the copies that we have and the original writings is not very large at all. This means a more accurate rendering of the text, as there is less time for copying errors to have seeped in. For the Homeric writings a gap of around 500 years exists, for Julius Caesar it is about 900 years. In contrast for the New Testament, the gap between the copies and the originals is less than 90 years, one fragment dated to 125 AD. This is less than 60 years after the New Testament is believed to have been completed.[96] This accuracy has been confirmed by the fact that many of the copies have come from wide ranging geographical areas without displaying significant variation in the text. In addition the entire New Testament could be reproduced just by relying on quotes found in sermons and other documents of the early church leadership.[97]

Probably the most significant piece of evidence came to light in 1947 with the discovery by a Bedouin shepherd boy of what came to be known as the Dead Sea Scrolls. These scrolls, consisting of over a thousand fragments of manuscripts, had been preserved intact in the caves around the Dead Sea, since right around the time of Christ. Examination of the texts has shown no significant variation between those manuscripts and the Hebrew version of the Old Testament from which the King James Version of the Bible was translated. What this means is that through the centuries before the invention of the printing press, when copies were able to be made only by hand, the textual integrity of the Scripture has remained intact. The Bible we have today remains overwhelmingly the Bible that was in existence twenty centuries ago.[98] Now while copies have remained extremely pure and accurate this is not to say that there has been no variation in the copies we have of the existent scripture. For instance the versions of the New Testament we do have, did come through the hands of countless copyists from many different locations in the region. Some variance can be expected. Critics have stated that there are as many as 200,000 mistakes found in the copies we have. The implication of course is that the Bible as we know is an unreliable document. If there is no consistency in the Scripture itself, it cannot possibly represent some form of absolute truth. The critics' claims however do not hold up to scrutiny. The same word misspelled in each of a thousand different manuscripts was counted as a thousand errors. Other 'errors', may include inadvertently copying the same word twice, or the insertion of a word that does not alter the meaning of the passage. Another example of an inconsequential variation would be a change in the order of words in the original Greek. The Greek grammar being what it is, means that a re-arrangement in the order of words would not affect the translation. Now there are probably a few hundred variations that may cast doubt on the meaning of a particular line of text. But even in these cases, scholars have found that no article of faith or doctrine of the church was put into question. Passing through thousands of hands over thousands of years, the Bible has maintained its textual purity, to a greater degree in fact than any other ancient book.[99] [100]

Having examined the evidence, we can be confident that the Bible that we have today is overwhelmingly and accurately the one that was originally set down by its ancient authors. However, proving the accuracy of the text has little to do with the truth of the content. Critics still will point to the Scripture as being little more than an accurately rendered fairy tale, with little connection to reality. To them, this 'accuracy' at best proves that everyone pretty much 'got their story straight'. Their question – and ours – should be: Is the 'content' accurate?' That's the question we'll begin to take on next..

Historically Accurate !

If the Bible is but a fairy tale it is one with a catalog of confirming historical and archaeological evidence for both the Old and New Testaments. Repeatedly over the years, serious doubts have been raised about the historical accuracy of the events described in Scripture. Among the most famous of these issues had been the contention that, a whole people, mentioned dozens of times in the Old Testament, the Hittites, never actually existed. Now this issue has definitively been put to rest as archaeologists have found the records of this people in Turkey. Abraham's home city of Ur has also been found. Among the artifacts unearthed not far from that site, were examples of ancient Sumerian writings. These records speak of the dynasty then in power as being the *third one after the flood.* In another example, scientists have confirmed that not only did the cities of Sodom and Gomorrah exist, but were located just as described and ultimately suffered through a great conflagration. The discovery of the Babylonian chronicles substantiates the historical accuracy of the Book of Daniel. This for a long time had been a point of contention among critics. All records had shown that a man named Nabonidus was the last king of Babylon, contradicting the claims in Daniel that it had been Belshazzar. This of course cast doubt on the credibility of the whole book. More recent discoveries however have proved Daniel's claim correct. It seems Nabonidus took an unexplained hiatus from the throne without abdicating his position. This left Belshazzar as the de-facto king. Daniel was right. And archaeology has confirmed elements of 2 Kings regarding the rebellion of the Moabites. Literally thousands of archeological finds have repeatedly confirmed details of the Biblical narrative.[101] [102]

This becomes even more compelling when considering the evidence for the New Testament. Time and again Luke, author of the Gospel that bears his name as well as the Book of Acts, has proven to be a model of historical accuracy. This was found to be true even when confronted by the doubts of more modern scholars. Here are some examples. An inscription unearthed from an area northwest of Damascus verified Lysanias as tetrarch of Abilene. This confirms the contention of Luke 3:1 which had previously been questioned by some Biblical scholars. Luke's use of the term 'politarchs' in Acts 17:6 was similarly made an issue. Archeology later verified the use of this term to be accurate. Of course the point of this is that as more and more details are confirmed, the validity of the writing increases. If true in the small details, it is more likely to be true in the important message it is trying to convey. In fact, Luke's writing has been found to be accurate down to the prevailing direction of winds and currents described in the Book of Acts.[103 104]

Other writings too have stood the tests of the archaeologists. The Pool of Bethesda talked about in the fifth chapter of John's Gospel has been discovered complete with the five porticoes described. Also found were the Pool of Siloam and Jacob's Well.[105] The ossuary of Caiaphas, who played such a prominent role in the trial of Jesus, along with an inscription referring to Pontius Pilate, is on display at the Israeli Museum in Jerusalem. Inscriptions on Christian burial memorials referring to Jesus as Lord, and 'Jesus Christ the Redeemer' have been found dating back to as little as 10 years after the crucifixion. This testifies to the fact that even at that early date Christ was being accepted as the Son of God. This was not, as some critics have asserted, a later invention that crept in over the centuries. The name of Simon of Cyrene, mentioned in Marks's Gospel as the man put into service to help Jesus to carry the cross is found on yet another ossuary. Finally, and most eerily perhaps, a discovery was made in a cave just off the Bethany road and near the site of that village. Again found on ossuaries, along with the sign of the cross were three very familiar names from the gospels; those of Martha, Mary and Lazarus whom Jesus called back to life.[106]

If archaeology has been helpful in establishing the historical accuracy of the Bible, the evidence of ancient history has provided even more confirming evidence. One of the keys to testing the historical accuracy of the New Testament is dating the gospels. If indeed they were written long after Jesus death that would allow time for inaccuracies and mythical elements to creep into the accounts. What we find though is that the speculations of some in years past, that the gospels were written in the second century or later holds very little water. Even in liberal circles now, the dating of the gospels runs to about 90 - 100 AD. This is still within the lifetimes of Jesus' contemporaries. These witnesses would have either corroborated or contradicted the gospel accounts. A movement based upon the resurrection of Christ from the dead, and using for evidence his crucifixion and his miracles, would have had a hard time generating any momentum if it was being successfully contradicted in its most basic facts.

But more careful scholarship has put the writing of the gospel accounts at an even earlier point in history. After reexamining the evidence, Cambridge scholar Dr. John Robinson believes they were completed by AD 64, less than a generation after Christ's death. Archaeologist Dr. William Albright dates them at between 50 and 75 AD. Scholars point to the abrupt ending of the Book of Acts, Luke's second work, and the failure of any New Testament writings to mention the destruction of the Temple at Jerusalem in the year 70. The silence of the gospels on this event would have been strange indeed had they been written after the temple was destroyed. As Grant Jeffrey states in his book, 'Jesus The Great Debate'; "The silence of the Gospels about this tragic fulfillment of Christ's prophecy provides convincing evidence to any unbiased observer that the Gospel writers must have written their manuscripts at some point prior to the Jewish-Roman War in AD 66-70." Because we find portions of Mark's gospel in Luke's work, we know that it must have been written earlier than that. Further, the writing of the major epistles of Paul pre-dated even these earliest Gospels, dating back to the 40's and 50's. Contained in those works are clear unambiguous statements of the divinity of Christ and the saving nature of his death and resurrection.

Now there is good evidence that belief in the resurrection can be documented back to within two years of the crucifixion. Almost all of the witnesses would still have been alive. It would have been impossible for this new movement to have grown up in Jerusalem, where so much of its history had taken place, if the Christian message had been based on distortions or outright lies. In fact opponents of nascent Christianity never claimed that the miracles of

Jesus did not happen. In the face of the thousands of witnesses to his teaching and his many works, they could not do so. There was no room here for the encroachments of mythology.[107] [108]

Testing the Authors

When considering the gospel writers or the record of the apostles in general, we see a group that had little to gain and certainly much to lose by promoting this new religion. By their own testimony they were flawed, weak men. Peter denied Jesus three times during the crisis of his ministry. The others seem to have abandoned Christ completely at his time of trial. Yet not having understood why Jesus had to die, just a short time after his crucifixion they were speaking out boldly for the truth of his resurrection from the dead. They did so in the face of institutional opposition that they knew was not beyond seeking their very lives. And to what gain? There was no financial gain. None of them got rich. To the contrary, many faced persecution wherever they went.

Look at it this way. While Jesus was with them during His ministry, the twelve Apostles would be evaluated on the world's standards as pretty much a bunch of losers. James and John tried to set aside for themselves the choice places of power and prestige in the Kingdom. (Mark 10:35-37, Matthew 20:20-21) Peter could walk on water and was the first to recognize that Jesus was — *"the Christ, the Son of the living God."* Yet just minutes later Peter sustained a stinging rebuke from Jesus for trying to divert Him from the purpose of His ministry; - our Lord saying: "*Get behind Me, Satan! You are an offense to Me" (*Matthew 16:13-23) During Christ's trial, Peter denied Him three times. Most of the other's just ran away. In sum, Jesus' closest disciples were; weak, vacillating and scheming. They had been witnesses to His many signs and wonders, His healings, His mastery over nature. Still their faith failed. Then something changed. They saw the risen Christ! It was the Resurrection that changed them. They had seen Jesus beat the very forces of death, fulfilling the ancient prophecies.

They were witnesses to His crucifixion and burial. But once they had seen Him, and touched Him, and eaten with Him, and later received the Holy Spirit, - they were transformed. The Truth was alive in them. They witnessed the martyrdom of many contemporaries of their movement. Yet they persisted. And when they preached they called as witnesses the people to which they spoke. In their message they pointed to the public miracles Christ had performed. And the movement grew because the people knew that evidence first hand.

They sought no position, no monetary gain. There was no plausible motivation for lying. Not even torture or the threat of death could shake their resolve. Save for John, who survived a boiling in oil, all the remaining Apostles went to their deaths proclaiming the reality of Jesus and His message. Peter was crucified in Rome, - upside down. Nathaniel was whipped to death in Armenia. Andrew hung on a cross for two days, preaching to his executioners all the while. Thomas was speared to death in India. Jesus' brother James, (not an apostle but a major church leader), was thrown from the top of the Temple and then beaten to death with a club. Matthew was martyred in Ethiopia, Gospel author Mark was dragged by horses through the streets of Alexandria, Egypt. James the son of Zebedee was beheaded in Jerusalem, his example serving to convert the officer that accompanied him to his death. Almost all could have saved their lives by recanting their Faith. None would. Would they have given their lives so willingly to follow a lie? No! The authors of those documents were convinced of the truth of the Gospel. Jesus is risen![109] They knew that the Truth was even more powerful than death. Christ had vanquished that impostor.

There is something else. 'The Faith' Grew Up In Jerusalem. Christianity was born right there where Jesus conducted much of His ministry: Where if it weren't true, - it could have easily been destroyed. After the claimed Resurrection the authorities could have produced the body and put an end to the young movement. They didn't: Because they couldn't! If the apostles were telling lies, the Christian Faith could have never got off the ground. But it did. In fact it grew by leaps and bounds in the face of violent opposition from both the Jewish and Roman authorities.

Not two months after Christ's Resurrection, Peter relied on the very fact that Jesus' ministry and miracles were publicly performed in Jerusalem. *"Men of Israel, listen to this: Jesus of Nazareth was a man accredited by God to you by miracles, wonders and signs, which God did among you through him, as you yourselves know."* (Acts 2:22) The miracles of the recently crucified Christ could serve as a tool only because they were so widely known and accepted by the populace. *"As you yourselves know,"* said Peter in addressing the crowd. Jesus' miracles were not denied by His enemies because they could not be. Even non-believers had witnessed Christ's wide mastery over the forces of nature.

Paul later used the widely known and attested fact of Christ's rising as evidence to the skeptics of his day. In his letter to the Corinthians, Paul in effect challenged his readers to check out the evidence by naming some of those who witnessed the risen Christ. "*He was seen by Cephas, then by the twelve. After that He was seen by over five hundred brethren at once, of whom the greater part remain to the present, but some have fallen asleep. After that He was seen by James, then by all the apostles."* (1Corinthians 15:5-7) Paul was naming names; saying in effect: 'You go talk to them!'

CHAPTER 7
TESTING PROPHECY

Time and again the Bible has been put to the test. Whether relying on archaeology, the testimony of history or considering its internal consistency, it has always passed that test. But the Bible must be judged on even a more stringent standard than other works of antiquity if it is to be considered what it claims to be, the very word of God. Throughout its 66 books the Bible makes numerous prophetic claims. These are not general or elusive in nature. These claims may not be easily misinterpreted, but are rather specific and testable predictions. The Bible invites us to test the words of its' prophets. It tells us to ask 'Was it accurate?' 'Did it come true?' Jeremiah 28:9 says, "But the prophet who prophesies peace will be recognized as one truly sent by the Lord only if his prediction comes true." And Deuteronomy18:22 states, 'If what a prophet proclaims in the name of the Lord does not take place or come true, that is a message the Lord has not spoken." Scripture itself has set the standard high. Only if it is true can it be from God. And only if it is true and from God can we put our full faith onto it as the anchor of our world-view.

TESTING PROPHECY

In looking at the prophecies of the Old Testament, we find they can be divided into three broad categories. These would include, general historical prophecies, prophecies concerning the nation of Israel, and those dealing with the coming of the Messiah. (24) In the first category, one of the most striking predictions concerns the fate of Babylon. Chapters 13 and 14 in Isaiah and especially Jeremiah 51 predicted the downfall of that empire in detail. Jeremiah foretold its' destruction by the Medes out of the north, the return of the captive nations to their lands and the fact that the land would remain desolate forever. History has confirmed that prediction. Another example of a fulfilled historical prediction concerns the destruction of the city of Tyre. Written hundreds of years before the event, Ezekiel 26 foresaw the complete annihilation of that city. *"I am going to bring against Tyre Nebuchadnezzar king of Babylon, king of kings, with horses, with horsemen and a great army….they will break down your walls and demolish your fine houses and throw your stones, timber and rubble into the sea."* (Ezekiel 26:7&12) This too came to pass exactly as predicted. Nebuchadnezzar did destroy the city. Later Alexander the Great built a causeway from the rubble to the island where the survivors had fled, by throwing the remainder of houses and walls into the sea. That causeway remains to this day. (25)

As to the prophecies concerning the nation of Israel, the accuracy is astounding. Here are just a few examples. The outline of the history of the Jewish people for the last 2000 years or so is generally known. For centuries the Jews were scattered among all the nations of the world, yet somehow retaining their own separate culture. Then in 1948 an unheard of thing happened, the nation of Israel was reborn. Not only did it come back into existence, but it did so in one day by a proclamation on May 14th of that year. Now thousands of years ago, Hosea, the Old Testament prophet wrote, *"My God will reject them because they have not obeyed him; they will be wanderers among the nations."* (Hosea 9:17) In Deuteronomy 28:25 we read that Israel will be defeated and flee in seven different directions. But the Bible predicts not just the dispersion of the nation but its eventual rebirth. Ezekiel 38:8 talks about a land, *"In future years… whose people were gathered from many nations to the mountains of Israel, which had long been desolate."* Micah 5:3 tells us, *"Therefore Israel will be abandoned until the time when she who is in labor gives birth and the rest of his brothers return to join the Israelites."* And seemingly in answer to this we read in Isaiah 66:8, *"Who has ever heard of such a thing? Who has ever seen such things? Can a country be brought forth in a day, or a nation brought forth in a moment?"* This chain of events is unprecedented in history that a people defeated in war and scattered not only survived centuries of dispersion without a homeland but actually became a nation again. Dozens of nations of the ancient world have long since disappeared, once suffering catastrophic defeat, as did Israel after the war with Rome ending in AD 70. Yet somehow Israel survived and was reborn, resurrected. It defies credulity.

****　　****

Those are some of the more general prophecies found in the Old Testament. Now let's look at the Messianic Prophecies; those concerning the coming of Messiah, Jesus. These were all written hundreds of years before the birth of Christ, yet in their precision and detail they can unmistakably refer only to the life of one man; Jesus of Nazareth. Some have suggested that Jesus, being a man with a 'messiah complex', arranged his life to have fulfilled these prophecies in order to prove He was the promised Savior. While it is true that Christ may have been able to have arranged some of his actions to conform to the predictions of scripture, so many more were entirely out of his control. The laws of probability tell us this is no matter of mere chance.

The Messianic Prophecies

The Messiah would come from the tribe of Judah

[Genesis 49:10] – Written: 1400 BC. Fulfilled: At Jesus' birth. Even later 1st century AD Jewish authorities acknowledged that Jesus was from the tribe of Judah and the House of David. In other words they acknowledged that He was, in those respects, qualified to be their King.

The Messiah would be born in Bethlehem

[Micah 5:2] – Written between 750-686 BC. Fulfilled: At Christ's birth. Passage: *"But you, Bethlehem Ephrathah,Though you are little among the thousands of Judah, Yet out of you shall come forth to Me The One to be Ruler in Israel, Whose goings forth are from of old, From everlasting."*

Betrayed by a friend

[Psalm 41:9] – Written: Circa 1000 BC. Fulfilled: Most are familiar with the passages describing the last supper in Luke 22:3-4 & John 13:18, when his disciple Judas dipped the bread with Jesus before going out to betray Him. Passage: *"Even my own familiar friend in whom I trusted, Who ate my bread, Has lifted up his heel against me."*

Jesus to be betrayed for 30 pieces of silver, and the money spent on a "potter's field."

[Zechariah 11:12-13] – Written circa 520 BC. Fulfilled: Matthew 26:14-15 tells us: *"Then one of the twelve, called Judas Iscariot, went to the chief priests and said, 'What are you willing to give me if I deliver Him to you?' And they counted out to him thirty pieces of silver."* After Jesus was condemned to die, Judas brought the money back to the High Priests and threw it into the Temple. Matthew 26:6-7 describes what the Jewish authorities did with that blood money. *"And the chief priests took the silver pieces, and said, It is not lawful for to put them into the treasury, because it is the price of blood. And they took counsel, and bought with them the potter's field, to bury strangers in."* Here's the prophecy that was fulfilled found in Zechariah 11:12-13: *"'If it is agreeable to you, give me my wages; and if not, refrain.' So they weighed out for my wages thirty pieces of silver. And the LORD said to me, 'Throw it to the potter—that princely price they set on me.' 'So I took the thirty pieces of silver and threw them into the house of the LORD for the potter.'"*

The Christ would enter Jerusalem on a donkey

[Zechariah 9:9] – Written about 500 years before Christ. Fulfilled by Jesus when He entered in triumph on Palm Sunday.

The disciples scatter when Jesus is taken

[Zechariah 13:7] – Fulfilled in the Garden of Gethsemane. The apostles ran off as Jesus was seized. The passage reads in part: *"Strike the Shepherd that the sheep may be scattered."*

Jesus would be struck and spit on

[Isaiah 50:6] – Passage: *"I gave My back to those who strike Me, And My cheeks to those who pluck out the beard; I did not cover My face from humiliation and spitting."* Matthew 27:30 records the fulfillment of that prophecy. *"I gave My back to those who strike Me, And My cheeks to those who pluck out the beard; I did not cover My face from humiliation and spitting."*

His death by crucifixion; hundreds of years before that method of death was used

[Psalm 22:16] – Passage: *"They pierced My hands and My feet."* Fulfillment: On the Cross.

They would divide and gamble for the rights to His clothing

[Psalm 22:18] – Passage: *"They divide my garments among them, And for my clothing they cast lots."* John 19:23-24 describes how after they hung Him on the Cross, the Roman soldiers divided his clothing and gambled for His seamless tunic.

Messiah's Mission: To suffer and die bearing the sins of all that would accept Him

[Isaiah 52:13-53:12] – Written around 700 BC – Fulfilled: In the details of the ministry, suffering and crucifixion of Christ. That passage tells us that He will bear the sin of *"many nations"* as He was *"wounded for our transgressions"* and *"bruised for our iniquities…And by His stripes we are healed."* In Isaiah 53:7 it tells us "*He opened not His mouth, He was led as a lamb to the slaughter.*" Later we find that at His trial He was silent before Pilate, not attempting to defend Himself though it cost Him His life. It tells us also that He would be executed *"with the wicked"* (the 2 thieves on the cross), and buried *"with the rich at His death,"* which He was. The Christ would be *"numbered with the Transgressors"* yet He *"bore the sins of many."* That passage tells us that He would be rejected yet make "*His soul an offering for sin.*" In the end, God will raise Him up with *"the great"* because "*He poured out His soul unto death.*"

And there are others

Psalm 69:21 predicted that they would give Him vinegar to drink. They did. – Psalm 34:20 recorded how none of His bones would be broken. They weren't. – Zechariah 12:10 prophesied that He would be pierced. He was pierced by a Roman soldier to make sure He was dead. – Psalm 35:11 speaks of the false witnesses that would testify against Him. – Psalm 55:12-14 tells us that He would be betrayed by a friend. *"For it is not an enemy who reproaches me … But it is you, a man my equal, My companion and my familiar friend. We who had sweet fellowship together, Walked in the house of God in the throng."* There are others still.

WORLD-VIEW IMPLICATIONS

So we have seen the Bible put to the test and found that the Bible is unlike any of the other ancient 'holy' books in that it makes truth claims and proclamations that can be tested against reality. [And in fact there is a prophecy found in the 9th chapter of the Book of Daniel that accurately predicted Jesus arrival as Messiah down to the exact day. We'll deal with that prophecy in the next section of the book.] Time and again it has been subjected to the exacting standards of modern scholarship. It has not been found wanting.

The Bible, taken as an entire work, is a document of remarkable coherence and thematic unity. Its seeming contradictions are often easily cleared up just by studying them in context, and interpreting them in the light of other unambiguous passages of Scripture. Its unity is evident when we look at the way it approaches the core issues of life so consistently throughout each of its' 66 books. The coherence of its' message is apparent in its' teachings about the nature of God, the character of man, the need for salvation, and the availability of that salvation through the substitutionary work of the long promised Messiah. Through many prophetic passages it establishes clear evidentiary tests for the identification of that Messiah. Unlike the other 'sacred writings', found around the world it demonstrates a unity in the description and meaning of life which is unchallenged. It does so because it is a sacred work revealed through historical revelation. The events of the Old Covenant and the works of Jesus are historical acts, performed in time. The message they confirm rests on their historical truth. (34)

That historical truth has been attested to by so many modern discoveries in the fields of ancient history and archaeology. More importantly, while not every fact in the Bible has been corroborated, not one has been effectively contradicted. It is confirmed in manuscripts and inscriptions on tombs. It is reiterated in ancient writings, pagan and Jewish. It is validated dramatically by the fulfillment of dozens of prophecies concerning the fate of history and the coming of the Messiah. The precision and accuracy of the prophecy of Daniel is nothing less than breathtaking. In summary:

It is not a book of 'stories' and unverifiable myths, but accurate in detail as proven by archaeology, geography and history.

In the original manuscripts it is the same Bible that was given us thousands of years ago.

Finally it is testified to by the changed and ultimately sacrificed lives of Jesus' closest disciples. They gave all for that truth. The Bible is no fairy tale. It is not just a collection of stories 'selling' one view of life or morality. By any objective standard, by a preponderance of the evidence, it can only be seen as a remarkably accurate, historically verifiable expression of unambiguous truth.

PART III

THE IDENTITY OF JESUS

CHAPTER 8
RETHINKING MESSIAH

The Jews of first century Palestine were expecting their Messiah. The published translation of an inscription found on a stone in the days just before Jesus was born – published not long after the turn of the century - opened up the question of just what type of Messiah the Jews were expecting and just who Jesus was? So let's get looking.

RETHINKING THE MESSIAH ?

"Go your way, Daniel, for the words are closed up and sealed till the time of the end." (Daniel 12:9)

So here's the deal. Not long ago, there was a debate going on in Israel that involved n some level, whether or not Jesus, (Yeshua in Hebrew), - might indeed be the promised Messiah. It revolves around the work of an Israeli professor at Hebrew University, - one Israel Knohl, - and an archaeological discovery from early in this century and a stunning translation of the inscription on that ancient artifact. First of all let's establish just what we're talking about.

What was found was a tablet or stone with ink inscriptions from the period just before Christ. For years it was very difficult to decipher some of the writing but now Professor Knohl believes he has successfully done so; - and the resulting translation could transform what we know about what Jews of that time believed about the nature of their faith. As Knohl puts it, - (and he's not exactly buying into the Christian interpretation), - "The text changes the way we look at the historical Jesus, and provides a missing link connecting Judaism and Christianity."[110]

OK, we'll get technical – but just for a moment. Much of the debate between Judaism and Christianity, (originating as a Jewish sect believing that many prophetic Scriptures had been fulfilled by Yeshua), - centers on just what sort of Messiah was to be expected. Modern Judaism claims almost exclusively now, that what the Scripture called for was a triumphant Messiah who would rule an ascendant Israel. Now much of this controversy centers on the interpretation of portions of Isaiah 53. Let's look at Isaiah 53 verses 3 & 5. *"He is despised and rejected by men, A Man of sorrows and acquainted with grief… But He was wounded for our transgressions, He was bruised for our iniquities; The chastisement for our peace was upon Him, And by His stripes we are healed."* The now unanimous position of traditional Judaism is that the passage refers to the Jewish nation as a whole. The Christian one is that it is referencing the person of the Messiah come first as the suffering servant, and later to return as King Messiah. To the Christian, Christ's suffering and death as the payment for sin, is clearly visible in the phrase *"But He was wounded for our transgressions."*

In the rabbinic interpretation however was not always the case. Even the Babylonian Talmud written as late as AD 1000, held to the Messianic/(Christian) interpretation of the passage.[111] It was ultimately a famous French Jew named Rabbi Shlomo Yitzchaki, who put a definitive modern spin on the passage in the 11th century. From thence forward Jewish authorities have considered the passage to have in mind the entire nation of Israel. The Israeli paper Haaretz summarized it thus: "The premise that the Messiah died and was resurrected is considered the foundation of the Christian faith, one which differentiates it from Judaism."[112] But getting back to the tablet now, it is characterized as an apocalyptic vision given by the angel Gabriel. According to Professor Knohl, - here's what it says. The beginning of the inscription describes an End Times or eschatological war. Jerusalem is besieged and "residents are expelled from the city in groups." Then God sends forth "*my servant David*," to in turn send the Messiah Son of Joseph to give a sign heralding "*the coming redemption*." That's when it gets critically interesting.[113] Beginning in line 80 it reads "*L'shloshet yamin hayeh*," which is translated "*in three days live.*" And it's in the imperative case. What the entire line reads then is "*In three days live, I Gabriel, command you.*" So to who is this being said. The next line answers. To the "Sar hasarin" or "prince of princes."[114]

Knohl boldly goes on to suggest a link between the resurrection claims of Christians and 'Gabriel's Revelation.' He finds the link in the fact that the notion of a Messiah that dies and rises in three days is an established part of Jewish thought by the time that Christ walked the earth. In his mind, it was not just an addition of later Christian thinkers. According to Knohl, Jesus saw "His mission" was to be put to death by the Romans "so his blood will be the sign for redemption to come…This is the conscious view of Jesus himself."[115] Yehezkel Kaufman, yet another professor from Hebrew University confirms that thought, seeing the "*motif*" of the resurrection after three days as something "adopted by Jesus and his followers based on an earlier messiah story."[116]

Christian authors like Hal Lindsey have been telling us this all along. As Lindsey pointed out, many early Jewish thinkers were actually expecting 2 Messiahs; - The first, the Son of Joseph, a suffering Messiah, - and later, a Son of David, - or Messiah-King. Luke 4:16-20 records a very enlightening event, when Jesus goes into a synagogue and reads from the scroll of Isaiah. What's interesting is that Jesus is reading from Isaiah 61 beginning with verse 1, but then stopping in the middle of a sentence, - right where today we find a comma, in the middle of verse 2. Christ is pointing out the fact that the passage refers to the two phases of His coming. *"The Spirit of the Lord GOD is upon Me, Because the LORD has anointed Me To preach good tidings to the poor; He has sent Me to heal the brokenhearted, To proclaim liberty to the captives, And the opening of the prison to those who are bound; To proclaim the acceptable year of the LORD" Luke* 4:20-21 then records; *"Then He closed the book, and gave it back to the attendant and sat down. And the eyes of all who were in the synagogue were fixed on Him. And He began to say to them, 'Today this Scripture is fulfilled in your hearing.'"* So not only was Jesus claiming to be the very Messiah, but He also did something else unheard of; - He stopped quoting a Scripture in mid-passage. It was a signal as to what was going on. The very next words were clear reference to His 2nd Coming as Judge of the World. The rest of Isaiah 61:2 reads, *"And the day of vengeance of our God."*

The upshot of all of this seems to be that there is growing evidence that the Christian view, that the Messiah would come as a 'suffering servant' was at least present in some 1st century Jewish thought. And that at least some Jewish scholars recognized that there had to be a double manifestation of the Messiah to fulfill the Scriptures. So perhaps, this translation of this fairly recent archaeological find may open that discussion. Despite reasoned argument, Scripture itself tells us that the Jews retain a blind spot when it comes to understanding that Jesus is the Christ, the fulfillment of the Law. "But their minds were blinded. For until this day the same veil remains unlifted in the reading of the Old Testament, because the veil is taken away in Christ. But even to this day, when Moses is read, a veil lies on their heart. Nevertheless when one turns to the Lord, the veil is taken away." (2Cor 3:14-16) But there is good news in even this. That blindness will run its course: It will have its end. Paul explains it in Romans 11:25-26, when he writes, "that blindness in part has happened to Israel until the fullness of the Gentiles has come in. And so all Israel will be saved."

But now, unrelated it would seem to those archaeological finds, there are clues that we might be entering those times when the veil is being lifted and the times of the Gentiles may be coming to an end. In late 2017, the highly respected public opinion pollsters from Barna were approached to do a survey on Jewish Millennials living in the United States. That means those born between 1984 and 1999. What they found was little less than astounding. Jewish millennials see their Jewish identity as being more important to them than any other Jewish demographic group. In addition, three- quarters of them consider their faith to be "somewhat to definitely important" to them. Nine-in-ten consider their religion to be important. But now here's the real kicker. A full 21% of Jewish Millennials believe that Jesus was "God in human form who lived among people in the first century." That's an astounding development – that one-fifth of Millennial Jews believe in Jesus. They are aware of their heritage, somewhat steeped in their 'Jewishness,' – and believe that Messiah came – and that He is Yeshua / Jesus - the Son of God. And they believe this, despite the Holocaust, despite centuries of Gentile persecution (coming from those they perceived as Christians) – and despite the current world-wide rise in antisemitism. An additional 28% view him "as a rabbi or spiritual leader, but not God."[161] This follows the astounding revelation one year after the death of Rabbi Yitzhak Kaduri, one of Israel's most respected rabbis. In a letter opened after his death, Kaduri revealed his belief that Yeshua or Jesus was truly the Messiah.[162] While that shocked many of his followers as they along with the majority of Jews dismiss the claims of what they see as a Gentile God, we can still see that the spiritual landscape is shifting. Yet more scriptural prophecy seems on the edge of fulfillment. In the words of Bob Dylan, that great and honored Jewish-American songwriter: "The times they are a chagin'.

CHAPTER 9
PROPHETIC CLAIMS

Headlines suggest that a "Messianic Revival" may be in the making – in Israel! Congregations of Christian-Jews are growing and thriving in the Land of David. One leader of the movement talks of a new openness in Israeli society to consider the claims of Yeshua. There exist probably about 120 congregations with perhaps about 15,000 members; - a yet small number, but gathering in strength and influence.117 It was just back in 2005 that Rabbi Yitzhak Kaduri, in a letter opened after his death, revealed his belief Yeshua or Jesus was truly the Messiah. Still the majority of Jews dismiss the claims of what they see as a Gentile god. It was not always so. Remember, the Church began in Jerusalem, and was originally composed almost exclusively of Jewish believers. So what happened?

PROPHETIC CLAIMS

Prophecy pointed to him, this coming Messiah. The hope of Israel! The light to the nations! By the first century the anticipation among some segments of the population was palpable. The Jews were an unusually religious people. So much of their national life was centered on their sacred writings and customs. Yet despite the fact that the scriptures were so much a part of daily life, the expectation of just who the Messiah would be, and what He would bring, varied among the groups that made up the Jewish nation. Often this was just the natural response of people reacting to their own wishes and desires. To a large degree the role that the Messiah would play had become politicized in the popular mind. The yoke of Roman rule laid heavy on the populace. The hopeful eyes of an oppressed nation were focused on the prophecies regarding the ultimate victorious nature of the messianic office, rather than the predicted sufferings found in the same Scriptures. If their hope was misplaced it is understandable to a degree how this could be so.

The prerogatives of the Jewish leadership had been progressively usurped, culminating in the removal of the power over life-and-death from the Jewish authorities in AD 14. To the minds of many, a Messiah who did not confront and ultimately vanquish the Romans was no Messiah at all. This feeling would have been more pronounced in the circles of power, which no doubt, felt the sting of that loss even more acutely. The politicizing of messianic expectations undoubtedly contributed to the ultimate rejection of Jesus' ministry. An example of a contrasting result can be seen just a hundred years later, when the Jewish authorities put their stamp of approval on the false 'Messiahship' of Bar Kochba. Rabi Akiva signaled that approval by declaring Kochba, 'Messiah King', to tragic results. Thousands of Jews were killed when the Romans took the stronghold of Betar. The political nature of what was expected from the 'Promised One,' certainly was a major factor in the reaction to Christ by the Jewish nation.[118]

But as we've documented, it is not like the prophetic input was not clear. The claims of Daniel 9 were very specific. Micah told of his birth in Bethlehem. His miracles and ministry were written of in detail. Zechariah talked of his entry into Jerusalem on a colt. And once He had been crucified, it could have been confirmed that the circumstances of his suffering, death and burial were accurately predicted in Isaiah 52 & 53 and Psalm 22. To the many who would see, this was the expected Messiah. As mentioned before, there are hundreds of prophecies in the Old Testament concerning the coming and the identity of the Anointed One. Jesus did clearly match the identity of the Promised One in every detail. Christ was the unique fulfillment of those prophecies. What is possibly most amazing to realize is that so many of those Old Testament prophets probably did not even realize themselves the weight of their inspired utterances. 1Peter 1:10-12 speaks to their searching for the *"time and circumstances"* to which their revelations had led them.

Now all of the prophecies concerning Jesus were written hundreds of years before the birth of Christ, yet in their precision and detail they can unmistakably refer only to His unique life. Some have suggested that Jesus, being a man with a 'messiah complex,' arranged his life to have fulfilled these prophecies in order to prove He was the promised Savior. While it is true that He may have been able to have arranged some of his actions to conform to the predictions of scripture, so many more were entirely out of his control. Grant Jeffrey, writing in Jesus, The Great Debate conservatively figured the probability of anyone fulfilling just seventeen of the prophecies at one chance in 480 billion x 1billion x 1 trillion. This was not some easily arranged feat. The specificity of the predictions makes that impossible.[119]

Let's go a little deeper into just of few of the prophecies we briefly touched on earlier. All of these pronouncements found in the books of the prophets and the psalms were given hundreds of years before Christ walked the earth. These are no general pronouncements, but can be applied only very specifically. They describe in detail the birth, life and manner of death of the predicted Messiah. The Bible does set quite the high standard for itself. Recall that Micah 5:2 told us that Messiah would be born in Bethlehem. And from the Gospels we know that came to pass. Written approximately 700 BC this passage points not only to Jesus physical birth in Bethlehem, but also his descent from the line of David, also born in that village. But look at just the circumstances that were necessary to make Jesus birth in that location possible. In the second chapter of Luke we have the story of the Jesus' birth. In it we have the description of the specific census that made necessary the return of his parents to that location. We now have historical confirmation that return to an ancestral home was indeed required in census taking of that time. Without it Jesus would have failed the very first requirement of the ancient prophecies.

In Isaiah 40:3 we have the prediction of a *"voice crying in the wilderness, prepare the way for the Lord, make straight in the wilderness a highway for our God."* Matthew chapter 3 points to the ministry of John the Baptist as the fulfillment of this passage. John specifically talked about *"one who is more powerful than I, whose sandals I am not fit to carry. He will baptize you with the Holy Spirit and with fire."* (Mat. 3:11) Christ's triumphal entry into Jerusalem riding on a colt was predicted centuries prior to the event. Zechariah describes the Messiah's entry into the Holy City. *"Rejoice greatly, O Daughter of Zion! Shout Daughter of Jerusalem! See your King comes to you, righteous and having salvation, gentle and riding on a donkey, on a colt, the foal of a donkey."* (Zechariah 9:9) Fulfillment of this prophecy is found in Luke 19:28-40.

We have already seen the fulfillment of the prophecy found in Psalm 41:9. It speaks of the betrayal of *"my close friend, whom I trusted, he who shared my bread"*, referring of course to the actions of Judas. Zechariah 11:12-13 gave us in advance the details of Judas' betrayal of our Lord, including the exact price – (30 pieces of silver) – and the fact that Judas tossed the money back into the Temple - and its use to buy a burial ground called Potters Field. To any who are familiar with the story of Christ's death, this is a chilling fulfillment of the account found in the 26th and 27th chapters of Matthew.

When talking about the veracity of the scriptures, we noted the detailed fulfillment of Isaiah 53. It is probably the most important prophetic passage of the entire Old Testament that refers to the first coming of Messiah. So many of the details of Christ's trial, suffering and execution are found in that one chapter. Verse 7 talks about his silence before his accusers, and in verse 12 we see how He was condemned with criminals. *"He was pierced for our transgressions."* (v5) And in 53: 9, Isaiah tells us how He would be buried with the rich. In fact his body was taken by Joseph of Arimathea, a well to do member of the Council who buried him in his own tomb. Psalm 22 is another source of fulfilled prophecy. In it the psalmist foretells remarkable details of the crucifixion, confirmed in John 19. Beginning in verse 15 and running through verse 18, it reads, *"my tongue sticks to the roof of my mouth; you lay me in the dust of death. Dogs have surrounded me; a band of evil men has encircled me, they have pierced my hands and my feet. I can count all my bones; people stare and gloat over me. They divide my garments among them and cast lots for my clothing."* The story of the crucifixion is well known, and it was predicted hundreds of years before that grisly mode of death had even been invented.[120] [121]

The messianic prophecies I have cited are by no means exhaustive. Various lists can be found which mention many more. My point here was to show that details of the life and death of Jesus were predicted hundreds of years before his birth. The existence and importance of the Messianic Prophecies was known and appreciated by the Jewish scholars of Christ's day. In fact certain writings in the Book of Daniel point to a very specific time for the coming of the Savior. In order to understand the profound significance of the prophetic writings it is important to appreciate the expectations of the Jewish teachers living at that time. Those expectations pointed, among other things, to his appearance during the first few decades of the 1st century, the very time of Jesus ministry on earth. Jesus was expected, not least of which, for the reason of the prophecy found in Daniel 9, which prophesied the coming of the *"Anointed One"* down to the exact day!

So the real question then is this: What did the Jews know and when did they know it? Jesus was not just a blip on the tides of history. He was not just some man that came on the scene with no past and no prophetic perspective. There was a history here and a heritage that meant that the Christ; - the Messiah, - should have been expected, - and recognized.

What Did They Know and When Did They Know It?

Let's try and put this all in perspective. What can we really know? We know for instance that the testimony of his contemporaries confirms so much that we know about Jesus. A passage in the Babylonian Talmud, a Jewish book of commentary on the Scriptures, contains references to "*Yeshu, the Nazarene.*" Writings dated to the 2nd century confirm that He was hanged "*on the eve of the Sabbath,*" at the time of Passover. The passage also mentions Joseph of Arimathaea, who buried Jesus in his own tomb, and refers to the fact that He was accused of sorcery. This latter reference confirms the reaction of the Pharisees to his casting out of a demon that was described in Matthew 12. Other Talmudic passages speak about Jesus' disciples, identifying at least Thaddeus and Matthew and also speak about the powers of one Jacob who was said to have healed "*in the name of Yeshu.*" This is all evidence that his contemporaries never questioned the fact that Jesus was a performer of miracles. Instead opponents tried to attack him on the grounds that his power was derived from the devil. The public nature of his ministry meant that he could not be so easily dismissed.[122] [123]

Other historical confirmation comes from the pen of Flavius Josephus, a priest, Pharisee and generally trusted historian writing in the 1st century AD. Some of Josephus' writings include references to James the brother of Jesus and John the Baptist, whom he described as "*a good man.*" He is also known to have authored a passage specifically about Jesus, found in his work called 'Antiquities of the Jews'. Though long controversial, experts now agree that the majority of the passage comes from the pen of the historian. In the uncontested version he refers to Jesus as "*…a wise man …For he was one who wrought surprising feats and was a teacher of such people as accept the truth gladly.*" He goes on to talk about his death at the hands of Pilate and the fact that his followers believed him risen from the dead. Additional confirmation exists. Roman historians Tacitus and Lucian both testified to the execution of Christ under Pilate, Lucian adding that He was considered a lawgiver and worshiped as God. And the work of Caius Suetonius suggests that Christians were known to be able to perform healings and miracles.[124]

A most interesting confirmation of Matthew 27:45 is found in several ancient sources. In that passage Matthew writes, '*From the sixth hour until the ninth hour darkness came over all the land.*" Luke 23:44-

45 states it this way, *"It was now about the sixth hour, and darkness came over the whole land until the ninth hour, for the sun stopped shining."* Pagan historian Phlegon of Lydia, writing early in the first century refers to a "*great and extraordinary*" solar eclipse, dating it according to the Olympic year. He writes, "At the sixth hour the day was turned into dark night, so that the stars in heaven were seen, and there was an earthquake in Bithynia which overthrew many houses in the city of Nice." Tertullian found evidence of this in the Roman archives of his day. The Greek historian Thallus also wrote of that supernatural event, a most fearful darkness accompanied by earthquakes. Second century teacher Julius Africanus wrote that this was no eclipse of the sun. An eclipse is a predictable event. Working backwards from that time he points out that an eclipse is impossible when there is a full moon. This was evidence then that this unusual darkness not only occurred, but also was not due to an eclipse of the sun but was rather an unnatural event. 4 The Scripture too, prophesied that unnatural darkness. In Amos 8:9 written long before the event, we read: "'*In that day', declares the Sovereign Lord, 'I will make the sun go down at noon and darken the earth in broad daylight.*'"[125]

In examining the rabbinic writings, we find that the common beliefs included not only the fact that the Messiah was expected to appear at that time but that He was to be no ordinary man. They believed that He had existed since before the creation. The commentaries on Isaiah and Micah give evidence that it was commonly held that the existence of the Messiah was eternal. The text of Micah 5:2, describes a Messiah *"who will be ruler over Israel, whose origins are from old, from ancient times."* These writings also anticipated his cruel and violent death, the re-establishment of Israel, and redemptive nature of his ministry. Commentaries reveal that they believed that the Messiah would forgive sins because of his position as the "*Righteous One*." Their beliefs were based on ancient Scriptural prophecy and the commentaries on those prophecies. Both the Midrash and the Talmud itself reveal that the Messiah was expected to be the full Son of God. Confirmation of this is found in Psalm

2:7. In the King James Version we read, *"Thou art my Son; this day I have begotten thee"*.

In fact, predictions of the Messiah were so prevalent that it was the non-Jewish Magi, possibly originating from a class of Zoroastrian priests, who relied on the prophecy of Micah 5:2 to inform the unschooled Herod that the Messiah was to be born in Bethlehem. They too expected his imminent arrival to redeem Israel. Much of this speculation was based on the very precise prediction found in Daniel 9:24. The Rabbis of that era were aware that no matter how one interpreted the 70 weeks of Daniel, the arrival of the Savior should occur sometime in the first decades of the first century. This belief was confirmed by the teachings of the Essene community that gave us the Dead Sea Scrolls. They firmly believed that Daniel's prophecy would be fulfilled during their lifetimes.

After the destruction of the Temple in 70 AD all that changed. The later commentaries on the Scripture reflect the lost-ness and confusion of a people whose earlier hopes now seemed misplaced. Written after that time, the Babylonian Talmud acknowledged the prophecies of Daniel had predicted the coming of the Messiah, but that the time had already passed. Moses Maimonides, working twelve centuries later, recognized this too. Almost cryptically he refers to the censoring of that teaching by the Jewish religious leaders. He tells us they "*...have barred the calculation of the days of Messiah's coming so that the untutored populace will not be led astray.*" [They of course, were protecting the masses against the 'Christian Heresy.'] Grant Jeffrey, writing again in Jesus the Great Debate, cites some of the censored Jewish material. The writings confirm the basic account of Christ's trial and death. Significantly the passage also acknowledges him as a legitimate king of Israel in the line of David and most notably that He was referred to in the prophecies of Daniel.

There is little doubt that the Messiah was expected at just the time Jesus came on the scene. Events surrounding an obscure passage in Genesis accentuated the anticipation. Genesis 49:10 reads, *"The scepter will not depart from Judah, nor the rulers staff from between his feet, until Shiloh comes."* It must be understood that 'Shiloh,' by general Rabbinical concurrence refers to the Messiah. So what this is saying is that the power to rule, especially the power over life and death, would be secure in Judah until the coming of the Messiah. Throughout all the centuries of Jewish captivity this power had never been removed. Interestingly however the Romans had recently taken this authority. This happened on the occasion of the dethroning of Archelus, the king of the Jews in AD 14. This would have been the same year that Jesus came up to the temple for his Bar Mitzvah at the age of twelve. In his commentary Rabbi Rachmon describes the consternation of the assembly when this power was removed. They were mourning the fact that "*...the scepter has departed from Judah and the Messiah has not come.*"[126] So many of the expectations of the Jews regarding the imminent arrival of their Savior were based on the remarkable Book of Daniel. We need to look at that prophecy that led to such high expectations.[127] [128]

Daniel Predicts the Exact Day !

In Daniel chapter 9, written just about 530 years or so before the birth of Christ, the prophet predicts Christ's entry into his Kingdom to the very day. Check this out. Based on Daniel's prophecy, 1st century rabbis, those writing when Jesus was alive, - expected the arrival of Messiah right around that time. The Magi arrived seeking Him partially informed by a detailed knowledge of Jewish Scripture which had been gained by wise men and astrologers since the time of Daniel himself.[129] The Essenes, who produced the famous Dead Sea Scrolls, were another religious community that believed that the prophecy would shortly be fulfilled in first century Palestine.

Here's the prophecy they were all excited about, Daniel 9:25-26: *"Know therefore and understand, That from the going forth of the command To restore and build Jerusalem Until Messiah the Prince, There shall be seven weeks and sixty-two weeks; The street shall be built again, and the wall, Even in troublesome times. And after the sixty-two weeks Messiah shall be cut off, but not for Himself; And the people of the prince who is to come Shall destroy the city and the sanctuary."*

There are a couple of things about this prophecy which needs to be noted. When Daniel wrote this, Jerusalem had been destroyed. At that time there was no reason to believe that it would ever be rebuilt again. Secondly, Daniel predicted not only the rebuilding, but also the fact that this second Temple would again be destroyed. Of course as already noted, this occurred in AD 70 at the hands of the Romans. So in just the broadest sense we see that the prophecy was fulfilled. Coincidence? Perhaps, if the prediction it made was just a general statement. But as we read in Daniel chapter 9, we see it contains a claim of the exact timing of its fulfillment. The Jewish community of course understood the meaning and significance of its reference to the seven 'weeks' plus sixty-two 'weeks.' And for them it was this specific phrase that led to the widely held expectation of messianic fulfillment around the time of Christ.

Now the prophecy itself may sound confusing, so let's start breaking it down. Sir Robert Anderson, a former head of Scotland Yard and a Christian scholar first researched the issue back in the 1890's. He made an amazing discovery. So let's look at the timing: *"from the going forth of the command To restore and build Jerusalem Until Messiah the Prince, There shall be seven weeks and sixty-two weeks."*

Here's what we know: History tells us that King Artaxerxes Longimanus issued a decree to rebuild Jerusalem on the 1st day of the Jewish month of Nisan in the 20th year of his reign. Sir Robert Anderson used the Encyclopedia Britannica to begin his research, finding out just when King Artaxerxes came to the throne. It was simple to calculate that the day the decree was issued was the 1st day of Nisan, 445 BC. That correlates with March 14th of that year.

"There shall be seven weeks and sixty-two weeks."

The Hebrew word used here is shabuim,' which is translated into the English word 'weeks,' in this passage. By common custom we know that this word was often used to refer to a 'week of years,' or seven years in the Hebrew language. This is the context in which it is used here. Now there are to be sixty-nine weeks of years before the appearance of the Messiah. Sixty-nine *weeks of years* multiplied by seven gives us 483 years *"From the issuing of the decree to restore and rebuild Jerusalem until the Anointed One"* comes.

Now the first issue is, these are Hebrew or prophetic years of 360 days each. So Anderson converted the years to days; multiplying the 483 years by the 360 days required by the Jewish calendar. That comes to exactly 173,880 days from the issuing of the decree. Now the critical question becomes, when did the decree go forth? By turning to the 2nd chapter of Nehemiah we begin to get an answer to that question. That passage describes a command by King Artaxerxes Longimanus to rebuild the city of Jerusalem. This happened in the 20th year of his reign on the first day of the month of the Jewish month of Nisan.

The date of Artaxerxes ascension to the throne is even an easier matter. It can be found in the Encyclopedia Britannica. Counting twenty years from that date we find that day of the decree is fixed as the 1st Day of Nisan in the year 445 BC. Working through the astronomical calculations at the end of the 19th century, Sir Robert Anderson confirmed that this date fell on the 14th of March of that year. From that date that we begin counting forward the 173,880 days. What we arrive at is April 6th AD 32.

So counting forward from the 1st of Nissan 445 BC Anderson and the scholars who checked his work all came up with the same answer: The 10th of Nisan, or April 6th, AD 32. So what's so significant about that day? That's the first Palm Sunday; - the day that Jesus rode in to Jerusalem on the colt of a donkey to the affirmation of the praising crowds of Jerusalem. He was coming into His kingdom. We know from the Scripture that Jesus went up to the Temple to celebrate the Feast of Passover. Here's Sir Robert Anderson in his own words now. *"In accordance with the Jewish custom, the Lord went up to Jerusalem on the 8th of Nisan, 'six days before the Passover"*. Two days later, on the 10th of Nisan, (the date the prophecy indicated), Jesus made His triumphal entry into the Holy City. And Jesus came riding in on a colt, fulfilling the prophecy found in Zechariah 9:9

Now there had been more than one occasion that Jesus had refused the opportunity to be proclaimed King. This was the first and only time that Jesus the Messiah accepted his role of King and it occurred exactly 173,880 days from the day the decree was issued to rebuild Jerusalem; March 14, 445 BC.[130] [131] [132]

Confirming evidence can be found in the third chapter of the Gospel of Luke. Luke states that Jesus was about 30 years of age when baptized by John. This was the beginning of his ministry and Luke specifically identifies it as the 15th year of the reign of Tiberius Caesar. Luke specifically identifies it as the *"fifteenth year of the reign of Tiberius Caesar."* (Luke 3:1) That's an easily traceable time period. Scholars concur that this puts Christ's baptism in the autumn of 28 AD. That would put the final Passover of Jesus' three and a half-year ministry on April 10th of AD 32.

The Sunday before that was April 6th. The British Royal Observatory confirmed that date. So traveling this other route, through the history of the gospels, we arrive at the same date that Daniel did in his writings hundreds of years before. More than some vague otherworldly pronouncement, the prophecy in Daniel 9 turns out to be a precisely calculated mathematical prediction, accurate to the very day that Christ presented himself as King and Savior.[133] [134] [135] The precision and accuracy of that prophecy given to Daniel is nothing less than breathtaking. By any objective standard, by a preponderance of the evidence, it can only be seen as a remarkably accurate, historically verifiable, confirmation of unambiguous truth.

WORLD-VIEW IMPLICATIONS

What the Bible offers is amazingly accurate, verifiable and unambiguous fulfillments of dozens upon dozens of prophetic utterances that testify to an other-than-human origin for the words of the scriptures.

Ancient Jewish prophecies were fulfilled in detail.

Daniel's amazing prophecy of just when Messiah would 'come into His kingdom' proved accurate to the very day.

While other ancient holy books on the one hand, offered only vague and untestable prophetic claims of a generalized or untested nature – or on the other hand – predictions which have already been proven inaccurate – the Bible has been clipping along with a 100% accuracy rate.

CHAPTER 10
THE TESTIMONY OF HISTORY

We see how the prophets revealed with perfect accuracy and extreme detail many of the particulars of Christ's first coming. Daniel was given the means to calculate the day and Luke's gospel confirmed it. Now let's look at how the currents of history came together to work God's perfect will.

THE TESTIMONY OF HISTORY

Yet everything in history was leading up to this moment; the fulfillment. Steve Brown of Key Life Ministries points out the historical pattern. It can be found in the cultural mores of every people. The sacrificial system is found among primitive people, anywhere on the globe, at some point in their history. We see it in the ancient pagan cultures that developed around the Mediterranean. We find it in the New World cultures of the Aztecs and the Mayans. We see it in Africa and Asia. It is all tied up in the religious notions of all peoples, everywhere. It is as if God prepared the very thought forms of every nation to understand this. It is a universal notion. Without blood there is no getting right with 'the gods,' with God.

The God of Abraham revealed the sacrificial system through the Passover. It was the blood of the lamb without blemish that protected the Israelites from the plagues in Egypt. So it was that all peoples could appreciate the notion of sacrifice. It was around 1800 BC, that God, chose a group of ignorant desert wanderers, the Hebrews, and began to reveal to them the most highly developed system of "ethical monotheism the world has ever known." There is no explanation for this in purely naturalistic terms. Anthropology is at a loss.

The Hebrews, (and Hebrew means wanderer), were not a very sophisticated people in any other sense. Yet the supposed civilized nations around them, definitely their marked superiors in cultural and military matters, were woefully backward when it came to the development of a system of ethics. They were worshiping multiple gods and still sacrificing their children, or passing them through the fire, as the Jews were developing a scriptural and cultural heritage that pointed them to the One God of the universe.

For centuries, as the world wallowed in the practices of paganism, the Jewish nation awaited a Messiah, who, Scripture promised, would provide them – as well as the Gentiles - with a spiritual deliverance. This emphasis on the spiritual rather than the material was in marked contrast to the notions of the dominant cultures of the age. Notice the distinction too between the sacred significance with which the Israelites held their religious practices and the pagan practices of the nations around them. In the ancient world paganism was rife with the association of rampant sensuality, with the supposedly sacred. (Actually this is still present today in some forms of Hinduism, neo-paganism, Satanism and the New Age, - to name a few.) There were many examples of religiously sanctioned, wine driven orgies. The existence of the temple-prostitute-priestess was common practice across the pagan world. However, the development of the Jewish nation was different not just in degree but also in kind.

Now along about 700 BC the Greco-Roman civilization began to develop. Through Alexander, and later the Romans, it came to dominate the known world. Its' influence dominated the fields of art, architecture, writing and philosophy. With the conquering of the Holy Land by Rome, the notions of what became known as Greek philosophy was imported to that region too. Through military might and that ubiquitous philosophy that accompanied it, the world was united. And with the subjugation of Israel, the Romans had brought forth the intersection of those two themes of history. So it seems not by accident did the Messiah arrive at this time.[136]

This then was Jesus' world. It was a world of a captive Judaism. Any real understanding of the person of Jesus must necessarily start from the fact that He was a Jew. Further, we know that He was a teacher in the rabbinical tradition. As such Jesus used the technique, common to that profession, of question and answer to drive home many of his most controversial points. There are many examples of this in the Gospels. In Matthew 22 for example, He discusses whether it is lawful to pay taxes to Rome. (This was a hot and sensitive subject given the political realities of that day.) In Mark 10:17-22 He talks about what is necessary to inherit eternal life. The other technique we see so often applied is the use of the parable. These are found throughout the Evangelists' accounts. These too can best be understood in the context of their Jewish-ness. Many of them refer specifically to the religious history of the Jewish nation, especially in regards to their repeated rejection of the prophets. This theme is one justification for the inclusion of the Gentiles in God's plan.

Besides the office of Rabbi, Jesus also fulfilled the role and duties of a prophet. Christ spoke as one with authority. He claimed to speak for God. It is recorded in the Gospels that many times He began a saying with the words, *"Truly I say to you."* After reading the words of Isaiah 61:1-2 referring to the promised Messiah, Jesus claimed the anointing of the authority of the Spirit of the Lord by saying, *"Today this scripture is fulfilled in your hearing."* (Luke 4:21) With that claimed authority, during the Sermon on the Mount He called for an intensification of the commandments of the Law. *"You have heard that it was said to the people long ago, 'Do not murder, and anyone who murders will be subject to judgment.' But I tell you that anyone who is angry with his brother will be subject to judgment."* (Matthew 5:21-22) He continues in verses 27 and 28, *"You have heard it was said, 'Do not commit adultery.' But I tell you that anyone who looks at a woman lustfully has already committed adultery with her in his heart."* In Matthew 5:17 Christ makes an audacious claim. *"Do not think I have come to abolish the Law or the Prophets; I have not come to abolish them but to fulfill them."* Just three verses later He tells his listeners that in order to be saved, their righteousness must surpass *"…that of the Pharisees and the teachers of the Law."*[137]

But his audacity does not stop there. Significantly, Jesus goes on to claim much more. As documented in all of the Gospels, Christ goes on to assert not only Messiahship, but actual equality with God by being the beloved Son of God. Before we look at exactly what Jesus said, we must understand the momentousness of that claim to an observant, believing Jew of the first century. The pride of the Jewish nation is their unique relationship with and understanding of the One True God. His claim of equality with God spoke directly to the most central belief of Judaism. It spoke to the unity of God. The Scripture known as the Shema is the most important expression of that unity.

Found in Deuteronomy 6:4 it states, *"Hear O Israel! The Lord our God, the Lord is One."* This was the scripture ingrained in every Jewish believer since childhood. So even indirect claims that He shared in the essence of the godhead must have been greeted with some confusion among his followers and outright consternation on the part of the religious elite. Christ too, accepted the truth of the Shema. In Mark 12:29 we hear him respond to a question on which is the most important commandment. *"The most important one,"* answered Jesus, *"is 'Hear O Israel, the Lord our God, the Lord is One.'"* Now in the Hebrew the word used for 'One' in this case is echad. The word echad is used to describe a plural one-ness. It is the same word used in Genesis 2:24 to describe the union of husband and wife as constituting one flesh. In Mark 12:30 Jesus finishes his statement on the greatest commandment. *"Love the Lord your God with all your heart, and with all your soul and with all your mind and with all your strength."*

Geisler and Bocchino in their work, *Unshakeable Foundations*, render that passage from Deuteronomy with more of the sense that it would have had in the original language. It would read, " *Yaweh, our*

God, Yaweh is a plurality within an indivisible unity." The authors point out how, "*The law of God is based upon the nature of God.*"

They go on to elaborate. The law is not a collection of arbitrary commands but is rather, "*primarily concerned with relational harmony…. the plurality of God and the unity of God are both the standard and primary example of this truth.*" When Jesus uses this language from Deuteronomy to answer the question, He is not so subtly pointing to that plurality. When taken in context with his other statements on his identity, Jesus is arguing for the plurality that would include himself as a member of the godhead. The Gospel of John records for us another of those occasions when Jesus makes such a claim. Jesus is speaking with the Pharisees regarding his identity. They had asked him to answer directly if he is the Messiah. After chiding them for their unbelief and again pointing to his miracles as proof of His office, Christ speaks of those that believe in him. *"My Father who has given them to me, is greater than all; no one can snatch them out of my hand. I and the Father are one."* (John 10:29-30) Here again is that claim of One-ness in essence, while at the same time maintaining the distinctness of his personality.[138] [139]

Now to those familiar with the promises of Scripture, these reminders may have been just enough to see the validity in Christ's claim to be the Messiah. Inherent in the Scriptures is the notion that the Anointed One would somehow be an expression of the Divine Personality. Isaiah 7:14 tells us that He would be called Immanuel, meaning 'God with us'. And just a couple of chapters later in Isaiah 9:6 we are told that his titles will include, *"Wonderful Counselor, Mighty God, Everlasting Father,* [and] *Prince of Peace."* So any claim that He is the Messiah is tantamount to a claim to be God Himself. These assertions were of monumental significance.

Yet as we have seen, it was a question on the minds of the Pharisees, with a predisposition to disbelieve. It was also on the mind of Jesus' followers. Even with the incredible miracles they were seeing, drawing the inference that a man was somehow divine was not an easy step. These were Jews steeped in the Shema. *"Hear O*

Israel...the Lord is One." And this was a claim of such uniqueness and importance that even John the Baptist was led to question what he believed to be true. John, who had identified the approaching Christ as the 'Lamb of God', who had baptized Jesus, to his own dismay, and had testified that he had seen, *"the Spirit come down from heaven as a dove and remain on him"*, even he had questions. (John 1:29-34) Alone with his thoughts in the seclusion of his prison cell, this same John sent his disciples to inquire of Jesus, *"Are you the one who was to come, or should we expect someone else?"*

Jesus' answer is interesting in that He laid out the nature of the evidence to be considered when considering the validity of his claim to be the Anointed One. *"Go back and report to John what you hear and see: The blind receive sight, the lame walk, those who have leprosy are cured, the deaf hear, the dead are raised, and the good news is preached to the poor. Blessed is the man who does not fall away on account of me."* (Matthew 11:4-6) Jesus was pointing to the evidence all had seen. John was undoubtedly familiar with the prophecies of Isaiah and Daniel. Jesus was saying, 'open your eyes and see what I am doing.' This was his evidence for being the Messiah. Still, some will argue that Christ was just a *good man*, a *great teacher*; - that He never claimed to be the Messiah or the Son of God. This was just made up by his followers at a later date as a means of asserting power. But these are just empty claims contrary to the evidence.

**** ****

The identity of Jesus is the central question of all time. On it, hinges the salvation of all men and the fate of the world. But reason tells us He cannot just be a good teacher. Here's the claim in Christ's own words. *"He who believes in Him is not condemned; but he who does not believe is condemned already, because he has not believed in the name of the only begotten Son of God. (John 3:18)*

"But Who Do You Say That I Am ?"

Despite what the skeptics may claim, Jesus was not ambiguous about just who He claimed to be. Let's get right to the point and begin with his most direct assertions of divinity. Going back to Exodus God gives His own name as *"I AM WHO I AM."* (It is from the Hebrew pronunciation of this name that we get the word Yahweh, the Hebrew term for Lord.) This is the holy name of God. Isaiah 43:11 identifies that name with the Savior. *"I, even I, am the Lord, and apart from me there is no savior."* Now Jesus referred to himself in those very words on several occasions. In John 8:58 He is facing a crowd of unbelieving Jews. *"I tell you the truth,"* Jesus answered, *"before Abraham was born I am."* The crowd understood what Jesus was saying. The use of that term angered them so much that they wanted to stone him. Later John tells us of Christ's use of the term when He is betrayed and the mob comes to seize him. *"I am he,"* He declares and the crowd is knocked to the ground just by the power inherent in that statement when expressed by the Son of God.

Apparent in the meaning of the term, *"I Am,"* is the notion of the eternal. That is the intended sense of the term. Again in John we find Christ's personal confirmation of his claim. *"And now, Father, glorify me in your presence with the glory I had before the world began."* He is declaring not only his glory, but also the eternal nature of that glory.

Other assertions of his divinity were laid out in a series of statements in which Jesus assumed the prerogatives of God as laid out in the ancient Scriptures. As far back as Genesis 2:7 it was declared that God was the giver of life. There it was written that it was the *"breath of the Lord"*, that made man a living being. We find in John 5:21 Jesus' clear assertion of this power when He states, *"...even so the Son gives life to whom he is pleased to give it."* Later He states that *"eternal life"* comes from him, and positively affirms *"I am the resurrection and the life."* (John 10:28 & 11:25) Jesus also held that He could exercise the godly prerogative to forgive sins. He told a paralyzed man, *"Son, your sins are forgiven."* And to answer the objections of the rabbis and establish that prerogative He continued, *"But that you may know that the Son of Man has authority on earth to forgive sins..."* He said to the paralytic, *"I tell you, get up, take up your mat and go home."* Even in his assertions of divine authority Christ was not unaware of the difficulty of belief and provided evidence of his authority.

Other examples abound. In Matthew He spoke of his coming judgment of the nations referred to by the prophet Joel. John 5:27 justifies that claim stating that He was given that *"authority to judge because he was the Son of Man."* Elsewhere in John's account we find that Jesus said, *"I am the good shepherd"*, and *"I am the light of the world,"* (John10:11 & 8:12), both referring back to Old Testament passages. The claims of some critics that Jesus was just a great moral teacher but did not see himself as the Son of God are sheer nonsense. As we have seen above, the Gospels were written during the lifetimes of many witnesses to the events described in them. There was no chance for myth-making. Jesus clearly felt He was, and claimed to be the Messiah, the Son of God. No 'great moral teacher' could make such a claim if it were not so. Such a lie would automatically disqualify him as a 'great moral teacher.' Jesus said, *"I am the way and the truth and the life. No one comes to the Father except through me."* (John 14:6) He is saying, all access to the Father must come through him. The aggregate significance of all these claims taken together is weighty indeed. He was the forgiver of sins, the giver of life, the judge of all the nations, the light of the world, existent for all eternity. If He were wrong about any of these things He would be either hopelessly deluded or a deliberate liar. In either case, not the mettle of some great moral teacher. But Jesus was no liar. He followed those convictions to death.

Looking at the evidence it can be confidently said that Jesus truly believed himself to be the Messiah, the Son of God. But what of those who knew him the best? Peter, when asked by Jesus, *"Who do you say I am?"* replied, *"You are the Christ, the Son of the living God."* (Matthew 16:15-16) No more straightforward answer could be forthcoming. Thomas, seeing him for the first time after his Resurrection called him *"My Lord and my God."* (John 20:28) These were no mere words. Both of these apostles paid with their lives for holding to those beliefs. John's testimony can be found throughout the Gospel he authored. Paul converted from one whose overriding aim was the persecution of members of the new Christian sect to one who would eventually give his life for the faith.

The author of Hebrews called Jesus the *"...radiance of God's glory and the exact representation of his being, sustaining all things by his powerful word."* (Hebrews 1:3) The Apostles who had lived with him side by side during his lifetime all worshiped him as God, eventually giving their lives for the cause. In Matthew 14:22-32, we have the story of Jesus walking on the water and calming the storm. At the conclusion of that account we are told of Jesus' companions, *"Then those who were in the boat worshiped him saying, 'Truly you are the Son of God.'"*

But it was not just the apostles that bore witness to his divinity. Many of those who saw him preach or felt his healing touch also paid him homage. It would have been anathema for any Jew steeped in the Shema to have worshiped any but the One True God. Yet many saw Jesus as a member of that Godhead and did give him worship. (Significant too, is the fact that unlike his disciples, Jesus accepted it.) It began very early on. The second chapter of Matthew records the successful search of the Magi to find the Christ and worship him. Later we are told a leper came and knelt before him to beg for healing. (Matthew 8:2) A newly healed blind man worshiped him also. (John 9:38) There are many other examples in the Gospel accounts. Perhaps the most compelling, however, is recorded by Matthew. (Matthew 28:16-17) Speaking of the eleven remaining disciples, those same who had lived the better part of three years with him, witnessing all Christ had done, Matthew writes: *"When they saw him they worshiped him; but some doubted."* That last little note brings an extra ring of truth to the passage. Of course we can understand the human sense of uncertainty that must have crept in. This after all was the Jesus that they had taken their meals with, at whose side they had traveled the Judean countryside. Yet in the end we know that all these overcame their doubts and gave the most perfect form of worship, the work of their hands and the sacrifice of their lives.[140]

The pattern is beginning to become clear. The ancient Scriptures pointed to the appearance of the Messiah somewhere during the first part of the 1st century. Jesus specifically fit the identity of that Messiah as laid out in the Old Testament. He pointedly claimed that office and was accepted as such by those who knew him best. They saw his very life as a testimony of his holiness. Peter described him as a *"lamb without blemish,"* and quoting Isaiah 53:9 wrote of him, *"He committed no sin, and no deceit was in his mouth."* (1 Peter 1:19 & 2:22) John wrote of his purity in his first epistle. (1John 3:3) Jesus himself challenged his enemies on this very point. *"Can any of you prove me guilty of sin?"* (John 8:46) His question was met only with silence. Even at the trial that eventually condemned him, only false and contradictory witnesses could be found. This sinless-ness, this perfected moral character is one of the keystones to the validity of His claims.

This is not the pattern of saintly men throughout the ages. The Buddha, Mohammed, Gandhi, Isaiah, the great church saints and others were all overwhelmingly aware of their moral failings once compared with the perfection of the All-Mighty. Yet neither Jesus nor his enemies could ever find fault in his actions. A fitting apostrophe was put on this fact by a Pharisee and member of the Jewish ruling council named Nicodemus. Speaking for more than just himself he told Jesus, *"Rabbi, we know you are a teacher who has come from God. For no one could perform the miraculous signs you are doing if God were not with him."* (John 3:2)[141] [142]

CHAPTER 11

HE GOT UP !

But while the world may be ready at some level to accept the notion of signs and wonders, - miraculous cures etc, - if you will, - the notion of man that conquers the grave, - that rises up from the dead, - is a little too fantastic to believe. Or is it? Is this the final confirming and convincing evidence of God's power? We'll look at the evidence.

HE GOT UP !

What we know to be true for his many public miracles, would certainly hold true for the greatest sign of all, His resurrection from the dead. *If God exists: Miracles are possible*! And the Resurrection is the touchstone of the Christian faith. If Christ did not rise from the dead, Christianity is a meaningless exercise in good morals. The validity of Jesus' very message hinges on the truthfulness of that claim. Paul expanded on this in a letter to the Corinthian church. *"And if Christ has not been raised, our preaching is useless and so is your faith….And if Christ has not been raised, your faith is futile; you are still in your sins."* (1Corinthians 15: 14 & 17) The disciples were raising a very high hurdle for themselves. They were claiming not just some spiritual appearance that would have been so difficult to disprove, but they were saying that Jesus was raised in the flesh. If they were lying their opponents need only produce the body to shatter their claims. But they were convinced of the truth of the matter. They had to testify to that truth.

Now there are many critics out there that say that the resurrection is merely a legend, or a lie perpetrated by Christ's early followers.

But let's look at that contention. To what end would such a lie be put forth? Persecution and communal sharing characterized the early church. Its leaders sought neither fortune nor power. We know that Christians would pay for their lives for those beliefs. This was no lie. Neither could it have been a legend. This was the teaching of the Apostles just weeks after Christ's death. It is recorded in Luke's account of Peter's preaching on the day of Pentecost, found in the Book of Acts. If Peter was lying folks would have known. This was Jerusalem where the drama of Christ's death had recently taken place. Instead, 3,000 believers were added on that day, the Church's birthday.

We have already demonstrated Luke's record for historical accuracy. It is further confirmed by Paul in 1Corinthians 15:3-8. Scholars believe this to be a restatement of a very early 'creed' Paul received when he became a follower of Christ. There is overwhelming agreement that this creed dates certainly within 20 years of the crucifixion. Many scholars date it even earlier, to within a couple of years of Jesus' death. This creed passes on the very early held beliefs that Christ died to pay for our sins and rose from the dead again.

That passage reads: *"For what I received I passed on to you as of first importance: that Christ died for our sins according to the Scriptures, that he was buried, that he was raised on the third day according to the Scriptures, and that he appeared to Peter, and then to the Twelve. After that he appeared to more than five hundred of the brothers, most of whom are still living though some have fallen asleep. Then he appeared to James, then to all the apostles, and last of all he appeared to me also, as one abnormally born."* This passage, documenting so early the beliefs of the Church, contains several significant aspects that need to be looked at.[143]

Remember again that Paul was writing at a time when many of the witnesses to the events were still alive. By mentioning specific names and by claiming that Jesus had appeared to as many as 500 people at one time, he was inviting inquiry. Paul was so confident of his message that he wanted his readers to check out the evidence.

Secondly, and this is very important to understand, when Jesus appeared to Paul, he was an enemy of the Christian faith. In fact, he was consumed by a passion to stamp out what he saw as a dangerous heresy, if need be by killing off those who professed that heretical creed. It was Christ's appearance that changed the direction of his life. Here was an example of a hostile witness converted by the evidence.

Finally, in that passage in 1Corinthians, Paul is alluding to the fact that Jesus appeared to people in various locals on several different occasions. There are at least nine postmortem appearances described in the Gospels. This does not include his appearance to Paul on the Damascus road described in Acts. These appearances ranged from the individual, as in the case of Mary Magdalene, (John 20:10 –18), to much larger groups as in the 24th chapter of Luke. This was no will-of-the-wisp, no shadowy manifestation of desire or imagination. On these occasions He spoke with them; they ate with him and touched him.

Neither were these mere hallucinations. The appearances happened to different people at different locations and times. These were unconnected events, and not just to people expecting their occurrence. To the contrary, the disciples testify that they little grasped the meaning of Jesus' words when He prophesied his death and resurrection. In fact this was a truth that had been predicted, both in the ancient Scriptures and on several occasions by Jesus himself. In Psalm 16:9-10 we read, *"my body also will rest secure, because you will not abandon me to the grave, nor will you let your Holy One see decay.*" Matthew records Christ's prediction of his death and raising in chapter 16 and elsewhere. And Luke 9:22, puts it perhaps most clearly. He quotes Jesus as saying of himself, *"The Son of Man must suffer many things and be rejected by the elders, chief priests and teachers of the law, and he must be killed and on the third day be raised to life."* But his followers neither understood nor accepted these predictions when Jesus revealed them. Peter told him at the time, *"Never, Lord!...This shall never happen to you!"* (Matthew 16:22) It was not until after they had seen the risen Christ that Jesus' words had meaning for them.

And Jesus showed himself to both skeptics like Thomas, and outright enemies such as Paul. No, these events show none of the marks of hallucinations. Immediately following Christ's death, the disciples were a confused, cowering lot. They had run away during the trial and execution, and in the case of Peter had even denied association with the Lord. They were living in fear and despair. But in every case, the appearance of Christ became the catalyst for a radical transformation. Peter, went from on the one hand, denying his Lord to a servant girl, to on the other hand, preaching before thousands in just a matter of weeks. Paul went from avowed enemy participating in the mob killing of the martyr Stephen, to a tireless worker for the faith. The doubter Thomas was murdered many years later while preaching the Gospel in India. In every recorded case, those who reported seeing him after his death, became the committed witnesses of that truth.

Finally, if the Jewish authorities had produced the body, the early death of Christianity would have been assured. But they could not. The tomb was empty. There are a number of reasons we know this to be true. First of all, if the tomb was not empty, the apostles would never have been able to make that claim right in the city of Jerusalem, where the recent events had taken place. It would have been too easy to check. This fact is confirmed both in the writings of Josephus, and in the Toledeth Jeshu, a compilation of 5th century Jewish writings. Neither of these sources could be considered sympathetic to the cause of the Gospel.[144] Then we have Matthew's account of the events that followed the death of Jesus.

In chapter 28 he describes the generation of a rumor that the disciples had stolen the body. In his account he tells how the assembled chief priests and elders bribed the guards to say that Jesus' followers had come during the night and taken the body while every member of the dozen or so Roman guard was asleep. Of course critics can say that this was just Matthew's attempt to cover up the fact that the disciples did indeed steal the body. But that assertion will not stand up to scrutiny for several reasons. First of all, how could the guards possibly have known what was going on while they were sleeping?

Then there is the character and mindset of the apostles to consider. This was a cowardly bunch. Now, after the public execution of their leader, with the Jewish leadership and the power of Rome against them, they were supposed to have taken on the Roman guard, facing a certain and horrible death if they were caught, in order to perpetuate a hoax. And if they did generate enough courage, they would have had to find a way to roll back a stone weighing as much as two tons, moving it uphill just to get at the grave. They would have had to accomplish all this while not disturbing the sleeping guard. The final absurdity is that all of them in on this deception would live out their lives in support of this lie, not recanting even in the face of torture and death.[145]

To the early Christians, as unbelievable as it may have seemed at the beginning, the Resurrection was a fact. They were sure because they had seen the evidence. They realized the temporary nature of this life and the eternal nature of the next. The disciples had come to know Jesus as no one else. They had seen a man that was at once meek and humble and yet filled with courage and the righteousness of God. This was a man that would on one occasion, gather the little children to himself and on another take on the religious authorities, or chase the moneychangers from the Temple. This was a man who felt compassion for the multitudes, and at home in the wilderness. They had been witnesses to his many signs and wonders, his healings, his mastery over nature. They had seen Lazarus raised from the dead.

When at first they had seen him arrested and killed they were crushed and defeated. But once they had seen him, and touched him, and eaten with him after his death, they were transformed. So when the disciples died martyrs deaths they were testifying to the truth of the Gospel they had learned at Jesus' feet. They were affirming the reality of the miracles and the healings. When Peter died on his cross, or when Stephen or Paul were murdered, they were acknowledging the truth they had come to know.

So who is Jesus? He was a man of impeccable character. No one could find fault with him. Even the Jewish authorities that eventually put him to death, - did so strictly on the basis of self-interest; - as they scrambled to preserve their authority. As they, of anyone, should have seen, He was the fulfillment of prophecy. The Scriptures predicted the circumstances of his life, and the exact timing of his appearance. He acknowledged this and proclaimed often that He indeed was the Messiah. He performed many signs and public miracles as evidence of this. He healed as a sign of God's love. In His ministry He called for repentance and promised forgiveness of sins for all that would acknowledge Him and make Him Lord of their lives. He taught that He was *"the way, the truth, and the life."* And he promised eternal life to all that would come to him. He predicted his own death and assured them He would arise from the dead. And then to prove once and for all that He was indeed the Truth, He fulfilled that final prophecy and rose up from the grave.

WORLD VIEW IMPLICATIONS

The miracle of the Resurrection is one of the great wonders of history. There have been many legal scholars and men of letters that have set out to prove it a hoax, only to fall victim to the elegance of its logic. They have studied the evidence, beginning as enemies of the Faith. They have finished fully convinced that it actually happened.

In the 18th century, the English statesman, George Lyttleton set out to prove the Bible false and ended up concluding the Resurrection happened and wrote a book to that affect. The British lawyer Albert Henry Ross was a 20th century convert via the method of hostile study. He ended up writing a work entitled *Who Moved The Stone*.

One of greatest legal minds in US history was Samuel Greenleaf, the Royal Professor of Law at Harvard. His work: *Treatise on the Law of Evidence* "*is still considered the greatest single authority on evidence in the entire literature of legal procedure.*" He set out to prove the Resurrection was a fraud. Instead, in 1846, Greenleaf ended up publishing *An Examination of the Testimony of the Four Evangelists by the Rules of Evidence Administered in the Courts of Justice* that concluded the event had actually occurred.

Greenleaf argued that it was the Resurrection event that could only have motivated the Disciples to suffer and die for their faith. They believed that it was absolutely true. He wrote: "*As one after another was put to a miserable death, the survivors only prosecuted their work with increased vigor and resolution. The annals of military warfare afford scarcely an example of the like heroic constancy, patience, and unblenching courage. They had every possible motive to review carefully the grounds of their faith, and the evidences of the great facts and truths which they asserted; and these motives were pressed upon their attention with the most melancholy and terrific frequency. It was therefore impossible that they could have persisted in affirming the truths they have narrated, had not Jesus actually risen from the dead, and had they not known this fact as certainly as they knew any other fact.*"[146]

Then there's Dr Richard Lumsden, a biology professor at Tulane. He was a committed Darwinian atheist until challenged by a series of questions from a student. Suddenly unsure of the pat answers he was spouting, Lumsden undertook a personal research project to check out the answers. When he completed his inquiries he became a Bible-believing Christian.

Pillars of Evangelical Christianity Josh McDowell and Lee Strobel also started as unbelievers. However the evidence for the Resurrection in particular and the viability and veracity of the Christian World-view is both broad and deep and has convinced many of its most hostile – but honest critics.

CHAPTER 12
THE INTOLERANCE OF TRUTH

As far as the world system is concerned, we've made some pretty crazy truth claims in this book. Is the notion that to place our faith in Jesus Christ as the Son of God really a defensible position?

THE INTOLERANCE OF TRUTH

"I am the way and the truth and the life," Jesus said, *"No one comes to the Father except through me."* (John 14:6) On the face of it this statement seems to challenge the limits of arrogance and intolerance. How could anyone claim that He is the only path to God? A claim such as this one lies in direct violation of the supreme standard of the post-modern age in which we live. That standard is unquestioning tolerance. Yet the Christian faith uncompromisingly makes that claim and others like it. It claims that the truth it expresses is immutable and constant. But the world views such claims as intolerant and narrow minded. The post-modern world, concerned as it is with being fair and inclusive, suggests that the sincerity of the belief should be the test for the validity of an opinion. Reality is relative to the way one perceives it. To such a mindset, it becomes impossible to even admit the possibility of discovering objective truth. So all opinions are granted the same weight, regardless of whether or not they reflect reality. And if there is no objective truth, then any opinion that claims to speak authoritatively and exclusively on any subject, is by definition not true. In the twisted logic its adherents employ, the only position that is inherently untrue is the one that states a truth that is universal; one that is objective and exclusive.[147]

It is the contention of the post-modernists that the truth claims of one religion to possess exclusive truth, Christianity in particular, is not only intolerant but also impractical. It is impossible, they argue, that there is any neutral way to evaluate these claims. Instead it is held that no one religious tradition possesses the entire truth. Therefore all religions are valid. All possess the same value in our search for the divine. They propose there is one divine reality that the various traditions approach in different ways.

Underpinning them all however, lies the same foundation of similar moral values. And they cite as proof the transformational effects that any and all religions seem to produce in their adherents.[148] To them this is evidence that, in the words of Ramakrishna, the Hindu holy man, "*Many faiths are but different paths leading to the one reality, God.*"[149] In this world-view then, what really matters is sincerity. Any belief can take you where you are going. All of them are valid means to 'salvation,' which is ultimately universal anyways. Of course this line of thought diminishes the richness of and the differences between the various traditions. It reduces them to mere morality systems. The golden rule is found in so many of the world's religions. Doesn't that prove that on some basic level they are all the same?[150] This is the view of religious pluralism we get when all truth is relative.

But even the watering down of the various religious beliefs does not solve the problem. The tenets of the competing world-views reflect not just a difference in approach but an outright contradiction of the other positions. These differences extend right down to the most basic level, that of defining the nature of God.

To the monotheistic religions, i.e. Judaism, Christianity and Islam, God is an all-powerful personal creator. Each of these believes in the one-ness of God. On the other hand many Hindus hold to the idea of an impersonal reality which is found in all things. Others believe in as many as 330 million less than all-powerful gods. Holders of the New Age philosophies find god in themselves. (So do some Hindus.) It is an insoluble problem. The contradictions are very real. By the very fact that each claims exclusive knowledge, all religions are bound to contradict each other.

In light of these conflicting claims all of them cannot be true. Logically they can all be false. Only one of them can be true. What is true then is that all of them cannot have the same value unless all of them are false. With all respect to Ramakrishna, it is impossible that they are all "*leading to the one reality, God.*" One cannot include, in a system that says all religions are of equal value, religions that claim their own exclusivity. Logic doesn't allow it.

Perhaps it would be helpful to look at some of the characteristics of truth itself. Among its attributes, philosophers tell us that truth cannot violate the basic laws of logic. It is absolute and it is unchanging. By definition it is exclusive. Two contradictory propositions cannot be true. Jesus cannot both be God, (the Christian position), and not be God, (the position of Islam). There is no way to reconcile these two claims. They are mutually exclusive. As Ravi Zacharias puts it, "*Everything cannot be true. If everything is true, then nothing is false.*"[151] [152]

Let us review for a moment again some of the competing concepts of God. Christians and Muslims believe in one all-powerful God. However Christians hold that God manifests himself in three persons. Muslims see this as metaphysical sleight of hand and claim Christians are closet polytheists. Hindus think Muslims and Christians are about 300 million gods short of a full deck. Buddhists don't concern themselves with God at all. Those who hold to New Age beliefs think *they* are probably god. They just haven't realized it yet. Or maybe it's the universe that's their extended body. How are these competing concepts to be reconciled? According to the laws of logic they can't all be right.

Now the sacred writings of these religious works are not subjective. They are intended to reflect the realities of the mysteries of existence. We must take them at their word in so far as they are making claims about truth, claims about the nature of existence. If this language is dealing with issues of reality it is subject to the tests of logic, to contradiction. Take the Shema for instance. *"Hear O Israel: The Lord our God, the Lord is one."* (Deuteronomy 6:4) Either the 'Lord is one', or He is not. This statement does not leave room for the subjective opinion of the reader. Religious language expresses propositional truth. It is true or false. And if it contradicts the claims of a polytheistic Hindu, by definition, at least one of them is wrong.[153]

Evolving from polytheistic Dravidian and Aryan traditions, Hinduism must be viewed not as a religion but a religious system of related beliefs. There is no creedal consistency. Hindus may worship many gods or no god at all. There are no universal moral demands. Hinduism views man as a part of an impersonal divine force. All material reality is illusion. Therefore sin and even life itself is illusion. They believe in reincarnation. The uncreated eternal soul may be reborn thousands of times, living each time a life of suffering, until the ultimate release and union with the infinite. In each new life they pay for the karma of their previous life. They seek release from this cycle of constant reincarnation through either works, knowledge or ritualistic religious devotion. Hindus believe in many divine incarnations, especially of the god Vishnu. Some could even accept Jesus as one of these godly manifestations. But they often hold that God can be found through many paths, so they object to the notion of Christ as the unique Son of God.[154]

Buddhism is somewhat related to the Hindu religion. It began as a reaction to what its founder, Siddhartha Gautama (Buddha), saw as errors in Hinduism. He rejected the validity of the Hindu scriptures and the notion of the individual soul. He emphasized ethics over ritual and believed that the material world was real. Buddhists reject the concept of God. Like the Hindus they hold to the cycle of reincarnation. And all life is suffering. Nirvana is achieved when letting go of all desires. It is only through self-effort that this 'salvation' can be achieved.[155]

The New Age has much in common with both the religions of the east as well as well as ancient Babylonian rituals, nature

ıyiclubonline.com]
'M

NEW AGREEMENT EMAIL

3384

our contract are below.

DAN ZELASKO
668 2230

worship and the occult. Often the earth itself is viewed as a goddess. Probably the common underlying principal of the New Age Movement is that all truth is relative. Divinity is found within the self. One taps in to a personal divine potential by achieving a higher consciousness. As such there is no sin. Man is neither good nor bad, and all religions are essentially the same. This is of course a natural conclusion of any world-view that denies the absolute nature of truth.[156]

Now we come to the great monotheistic religions. Islam was founded by the Prophet Mohammed during the early part of the 7th century. A reaction to idolatry and rampant immorality, Islam was born amidst war and violence. The Prophet himself ordered the destruction of his enemies and united the Arab people into a vast army to spread the new faith in the name of Allah. While Muslims do accept the Torah of Moses, the Psalms and a Gospel of Jesus, the Koran takes precedence. They believe those earlier scriptures were somehow corrupted and are no longer perfectly accurate. In the Islamic tradition, Allah is a righteous judge. Jesus is a prophet but definitely of less importance than Mohammed. Unlike the Christian notion of salvation through the grace of God's love, Islam teaches that God has no love for the sinner. Everyone must work out his or her own salvation through acts of the will.[157]

So we can see so far that there are vast differences in the way the various religions view the world. There are many points of disagreement just among the eastern religions. Once we consider the claims of monotheism we will see that logic cannot support the notion that all religions lead to the same place. However, on the surface at least there seem to be some points of convergence between the great monotheistic faith systems. While we will see that they all disagree on the nature of the person of Christ, the question we may ask is: Is Allah of Islam the same as the Father worshiped by Jews and Christians. Muslims see themselves as part of the same heritage. They are 'People of the Book'.

But in his article, 'Is the Father of Jesus the God of Mohammad?' Dr. Timothy George points out that "*the way the Koran functions in Islam is radically different from the way the Bible functions in Christianity.*" He continues, "*in some ways [it] is more comparable to the way Christians see Jesus Christ- the express image of God, the Word (Logos) of God.*" For that reason the orthodox Islamic belief is that the Koran cannot be translated out of the original Arabic. Any translation does not carry the authority of the original. This reinforces the unapproachable nature of God, something held to by believing Muslims. This is in stark contrast to the message of the Bible; the universal love of God for all of mankind.

One reason for this contrasting view of God lies in the perception of just who He is. Just as is the case with Christianity and Judaism, Islam recognizes the fact that God is one. But the Muslim view is that Christians believe in three gods. The Koran makes this clear in Sura 5:76. Of course this is not the Christian belief what so ever.

As Christians, we believe that before the creation, before time, God existed in a community of love. If love is the supreme virtue, if God is truly love, then love must be inherent in His very being. Love demands an object. We see the operation of the Trinity; Father, Son and Holy Spirit, beginning with the creation act itself. *"In the beginning God created the heavens and the earth…and the Spirit of God was hovering over the waters."* (Genesis 1:1-2) Elsewhere in the Old Testament we see the Scriptures speaking of the Son of God. In the New Testament it is spelled out so much more clearly. *"In the beginning was the Word, and the Word was with God, and the Word was God."* (John 1:1) John is speaking of the Son, the promised Messiah. That same Jesus later promised us the Spirit, the Comforter, who will proceed from the Father and the Son. Again turning to the words of Dr. George, "*God, the father of our Lord Jesus Christ, is a God who has forever known himself as the Father, the Son and the Holy Spirit.*" This is the same God that came to earth to dwell among us, to set us free from our sin.

Now the Koran is known to have 99 names for the person of God. Not one of those connotes the notion of fatherhood. So translated into Arabic, the notion that Jesus is the Son of Allah is nothing less than blasphemy. Sura 19:88 is a direct denial of even a possibility of any connection with the Christian faith. It reads, "*Those who say the Lord of mercy has begotten a Son preach a monstrous falsehood, at which the very heavens might crack, the earth break asunder, and the mountains crumble to dust. That they should ascribe a Son to the merciful, when it did not become Him to beget one.*" And without that notion of fatherhood, so prevalent in the Christian concept of God, the concept of love becomes somewhat deficient. It is no wonder that the God of Mohammed is a God of judgment who hates those who do wrong. See the contrast. Jesus was the personification of God's love, entering human history. He brought not only the message of that love and the resultant forgiveness available to all, but He brought the message of himself. He was the expression of God's love; the love of the One God, living in holy community for all time; Father, Son and Holy Spirit.[158]

Despite claims to the contrary, the Allah of Islam is not the same god worshiped as Father by Christians and Jews. In fact, Mohammed chose Allah, (originally Alilah), from a pantheon of gods worshiped in Arabia. Alilah, was considered to be the chief god, the creator, at the temple of Kabla. In fact the god Alilah has ties to the polytheism of ancient India. There can be found in ancient Sanskrit, chants and praises dedicated to this god. Further, according to the Koran itself, Allah does not resemble the Christian God of love. While Christians know that God loves even the sinner, Allah is said to hate those who do evil. And instead of calling for repentance and offering forgiveness, the Koran calls for war against the unbeliever. Sura 8:68 states, "*It is not for any prophet to have prisoners until he has made wide slaughter in the land.*" And in Sura 66:9 we read, "*Prophet, make war on the unbelievers and the hypocrites and deal sternly with them.*" The Christian concept of a loving, forgiving God can in no way be reconciled with the Islamic notion of Allah.

Just as the identity of Jesus Christ is the stumbling block to unity between Muslims and Christians, so it is with Jews and believers in Christ. Though it is true that Judaism does not recognize the Trinity, and finds salvation within the Law; with the exception of Jesus there is agreement on many essential matters. Christianity, it must be remembered had its origin in the Jewish faith. Both profess a belief in a holy, just and righteous God. Both accept the Mosaic Law and the authority of the Old Testament Scriptures. Those scriptures have much to say about the expected Messiah. Devout Jews are waiting for the fulfillment of the promises they find there. It is the Christian position that they already have been fulfilled. In fact we see a 'type', or model of this fulfillment in many of the Scriptures and practices found in Judaism.

In viewing the Bible in its entirety, Old and New Testaments, we find a unity of subject and purpose. The message of the Old Testament is, 'the Messiah is coming'. The theme of the New Testament is, 'He is here'. Here are a few examples. In Micah 5:2 we read, *"But you, Bethlehem Ephrathah, though you are small among the clans of Judah, out of you will come for me one who will be ruler over Israel, whose origins are from the days of eternity."* This is a passage that is pregnant with meaning. First of all there is the obvious, the prediction that the Messiah would be born in the town of Bethlehem. We must remember that Joseph and Mary were not from that region. It took what one must see as almost a historical contrivance, a census, to take them there just at the time that Mary was giving birth.

Secondly, there is that last line, *"whose origins are from the days of eternity."* This is speaking of the existence of Christ before the creation of the world. Proverbs 30:4 confirms this notion of the Messiah being the eternal Son of God, *"Who has gone up to heaven and come down? Who has gathered up the wind in the hollow of his hands? Who has wrapped up the waters in his cloak? Who has established all the ends of the earth? What is his name, and the name of his son?"* Christ explicitly stakes his claim of eternal Sonship when He announces in John 8:58, *"before Abraham was I am."* The 'I am' in the Hebrew mean Yaweh, the name of God. It carries with it the notion, of the self-existent, an essential and defining attribute of God.

Finally there is the meaning of the word Bethlehem itself. In the original Hebrew it means 'house of bread'. So now we can see that there is both purpose and significance when Jesus speaks of himself as "the bread of life." In John 6:51 while teaching in Capernaum Jesus says, *"I am the living bread that came down from heaven. If anyone eats of this bread he will live forever. This bread is my flesh, which I will give for the life of the world."* The significance of this is the connection with the Passover bread.

In fact if we look at Isaiah 53:7 we find the meaning of the entire sacrificial system of the Old Testament and its fulfillment through the role of the Messiah's own sacrificial death. *"He was oppressed and afflicted, yet he did not open his mouth; he was led like a lamb to the slaughter."* Here was the sacrificial lamb of the Old Testament, the perfect lamb of the Passover sacrifice. Inspired by the Holy Spirit, John the Baptist recognized this when he saw Jesus coming and cried out, *"Look, the Lamb of God, who takes away the sin of the world!"* (John 1:29) Under the old covenant, the priests continued the sacrifices every day, trying to reconcile man with God. But Jesus is the Lamb of God. And Hebrews 10:10 tells us *"we have been made holy through the sacrifice of the body of Jesus Christ once for all."*

As Christians, we realize that the shedding of Christ's blood, the Lamb of God, is the reason for our celebration. So it is at the ancient Jewish feast of Passover. As the blood of the lamb protected the first born of the ancient Israelites when God visited the final plague on the Egyptians, so the blood of Christ protects those who believe in him, from the just punishment for their sins. In ancient times the sins of the people were laid on the sacrificial animals. Christ too has taken our sins on himself. The unleavened bread eaten during Passover represents the flesh of that sacrificial lamb. That bread symbolizes a new beginning, again much like the new birth that Jesus demands of his followers. *"I am the bread of life,"* Jesus had said. And at his last meal, a Passover supper with his disciples, as He passed that Passover bread He told them, *"Take and eat, this is my body."*

Now one of the cups of wine served at the Passover Feast is the cup of redemption. Taking wine, Jesus said to them, *"Drink from it all of you. This is my blood of the covenant, which is poured out for many for the forgiveness of sins."* (Matthew 26:26-28) The parallels between the concepts and fulfillment of the Old and New Testaments are uncanny. This is just a small example of the commonality of themes that is present throughout. Yet the stumbling block remains. It is Jesus. Without the acceptance of Jesus as Messiah, no other commonality is really significant. Jesus said, *"I am the way."* Judaism says 'He is not.'

So we return to the original question. Is it arrogant and intolerant for Jesus to claim that He is the only way to God? Do not all paths converge at the same ultimate divine reality? No, all paths do not converge. The truths espoused are not just different. They blatantly contradict each other. No amount of deeply felt sincerity, no strained attempt to reconcile, can bridge that chasm. With each tradition making essential claims that contradict the essential claims of another tradition, there is no logical way to be theologically inclusive. It is in their essential defining elements that we find no consistency. These are systems that cannot be reconciled. The source of their respective reality is different. And that starting point makes a critical difference. How you view the great moral issues of life will necessarily be affected. If truth is relative, if reality is an illusion, if you seek the divine within yourself, or recognize no divinity at all you will get one set of answers. If you look to an All Powerful, Loving, Lawgiver, Creator God, you will have an entirely different set of answers.

This is especially true of Christianity where the message is the person of Jesus. Among all the founders of the world's major religions, Jesus is the only one to have claimed divine status. He says, *"I am the way, and the truth."* Peter said of him, *"Salvation is found in no one else, for there is no other name under heaven given to men by which we must be saved."* (Acts 4:12) The claim is exclusive. It must be. Truth is exclusive. It was, as we have seen, a claim backed up by the fulfillment of prophecy. It was a title asserted through public miracles and healings. It was a truth ultimately affirmed by his own resurrection from the dead. The message is this. Man is lost and in need of salvation. All other religions can offer only the route of personal responsibility, self-effort and personal will as the means of that salvation. The message of Christ is much bigger than that. He offers the love of God. We are human and fatally flawed. Our efforts to reconcile with God can only fail. We know the truth. We know the law. But we cannot, and do not follow it. So God sent his only Son to pay the price we could not pay for our sins. He is the only way. And, *"whoever believes in him should not perish but have eternal life."* (John 3:16) Whoever believes! The offer is open to all. *That* is the *intolerance* of the Gospel.

Yes, the Gospel is exclusive. It claims there is only one way. You cannot come by sincerity. You cannot come by good works. You cannot find God through religion, not even some form of the Christian religion. You can only come through the person of Jesus Christ. He is the expression of the Father's love. He is the truth. And the truth demands a response. It demands more than just intellectual assent. The Bible tells us that even the demons give intellectual assent to the person of Jesus. They know He is God. The truth demands more than that. It demands action. It demands belief. It calls us to a radical, life transforming commitment to Christ. It offers eternity with God to all that accept Him. *That* is the *intolerance* of the Gospel.

CHAPTER 13

WORLD-VIEW IMPLICATIONS

TRUTH changes things. Once we get a new vision or a new understanding of how the world works our actions need to follow. Our choices and our behavior need to change. As we understand the ultimate TRUTH of God's world-view we become transformed. But choice is always involved. There is still the need to translate this new understanding of TRUTH into action. We are all faced with that ultimate decision.

WORLD-VIEW IMPLICATIONS

One day when Jesus was speaking with his disciples He asked them *"'Who do you say I am?' Simon Peter answered and said, 'You are the Christ, the Son of the living God.'"* (Matthew 16:16) For Peter that was a defining moment of confession and affirmation. He had seen for himself the miracles, and the ministry. He had heard the teachings and observed the character of the man Jesus. Now he followed that evidence to a decision. Because of that realization, that decision, his life would never be the same.

So much of this book has been an exercise in considering the evidence for the existence of God, specifically the God of the Bible and His Son, Jesus. It required no action on the part of the reader. But there comes a time when statements about the nature of truth require action, require a decision. Now, that evidence tells us convincingly that there is a God. There is a consistency in Biblical Christianity with regards to both its internal belief system and its correspondence with the nature of reality that is not found in the other major religious traditions. That correspondence with reality has its confirmation in findings in archaeology, history and science. This is a faith based on the cold facts of reality, built upon the truth. It is just as it claims. This is not a faith founded on contradictory logic or mystical wishful thinking. This is not a faith that says the sincerity of your belief is enough. It is the object of your trust that is important, not how strongly you hold to that belief. Would Jesus have so willingly died if it were just not necessary, if any path would do?[159]

We have approached the question from several different angles and it has pointed us in the same direction. Thinking philosophically about the nature of truth and reality we found that truth does exist and that it points us to the existence one, single source of universal morality. Even the presence of evil itself confirms our belief in an all-powerful loving God. We have followed the trail of the scientific evidence to find unmistakable signs of an incredibly designed and complex universe on every level from DNA to the cosmos itself. Along the way we noted the theoretical failings of the Neo-Darwinist model. When considering the claims of Christianity we established the credibility of the Scriptures. We noted the amazing accuracy of the prophecies and their fulfillment in the person of Jesus. He was the promised Messiah. Even the evidence for the resurrection was found to be extremely compelling. So when Jesus asks, *"Who do you say I am,"* we must take the question very seriously.

It is a question of more than just intellectual interest. Our answer defines our destiny. There is an offer implicit in the question. It is the point of the whole of the Christian message. It is as Jesus told Nicodemus, a Pharisee who had come to him to learn more about a man whom he recognized as a prophet of God. *"No one can see the kingdom of God unless he is born again."* (John 3:3) He was talking about a total transformation, a spiritual rebirth. For that is the offer that He makes us. He says in John 3:16, *"For God so loved the world that he gave his one and only Son, that whoever believes in him shall not perish but have eternal life."* Quite the offer! It is open to whoever believes. And to whoever believes He will grant a measure of that spiritual power that will enable this spiritual rebirth. The offer is not just to those that qualify in some way. It is not just for those that somehow become worthy of salvation. The offer is open to everyone, to whoever believes! There is nothing we can do to earn this salvation. It is the free gift of God. As C.S. Lewis so succinctly put it, it is not that "*God will love us because we are good, but that God will make us good because he loves us.*"[160] This is Christ's offer to each and every one of us.

"*Who do you say I am?*" That question demands action. Faith demands a decision. It calls for much more than just mental assent. It calls for commitment.

God is offering us the reality of divine reconciliation. And there is no price for this gift of salvation. There are no qualifying pre-conditions. God calls us to come the way we are, sinners lost in sin. We are asked to accept the gift of Christ on a cross, serving as our substitute. The Son of God takes on our sins and we are credited with His righteousness. Sounds crazy, but that's the offer. 'Here is my Son, kill him if you must. Then believe on Him and He will set you free.' God recognizes our sinfulness and our inability to do anything about our condition. He sees us lost in our sins. Even the best among us has failed to live up perfectly to the law. It is not enough to have done more good than evil. The law demands perfection. We have all failed. He knows our hopelessness. So He comes to our rescue.

"*But now a righteousness from God, apart from the law, has been made known, to which the Law and the Prophets testify. This righteousness from God comes through faith in Jesus Christ to all who believe. There is no difference, for all have sinned and fall short of the glory of God, and are justified freely by his grace through the redemption that came by Christ Jesus.*" (Romans 3:21-24)

That is the price of faith. Free! It is available to all who believe and put their trust in Jesus. That is the testimony of the word of God, the free gift of full pardon to us, the guilty ones. It is the love cry of the Father calling us into a family where we will always be loved, where we will always belong. By the blood of Jesus, the sacrificial Lamb of God, we are offered entrance into the Holy of

Holies; eternal communion with the God of the universe. We are offered the chance to become the children of God.

It's a 'come as you are' offer. There is no price for salvation, though salvation is priceless. For as Paul says of Christ in 2 Corinthians 5:21, *"God made him who had no sin to be sin for us, so that in him we might become the righteousness of God."*

Accept this offer! Surrender to Jesus…..and be set free!

END NOTES

1 Royal Museums Greenwich, http://www.rmg.co.uk/explore/astronomy-and-time/astronomy-facts/faqs/what-is-a-galaxy-how-many-stars-in-a-galaxy-how-many-stars/galaxies-in-the-universe, viewed January 22, 2015

2 What is a world-view? — Definition & Introduction, The American Scientific Affiliation, http://www.asa3.org/ASA/education/views/, Viewed January 29, 2015

3 Norman L Geisler & Frank Turek, I Don't Have Enough Faith to Be an Atheist, Crossway, 2004, pg 20

4 Dr Stephen Meyer, Does God Exist (DVD), True U, Truth Project, Focus on the Family,

5 Norman L Geisler & Frank Turek, I Don't Have Enough Faith to Be an Atheist, Crossway, 2004, pgs 52-53

6 Norman L Geisler & Frank Turek, I Don't Have Enough Faith to Be an Atheist, Crossway, 2004, pgs 37-38

7 Self-absorption as the root of evil behaviors is the general view of psychology. Example: Leon F Seltzer PhD, Self-Absorption: The Root of All (Psychological) Evil?, Psychology Today, August 24, 2016

8 Norman L Geisler & Frank Turek, I Don't Have Enough Faith to Be an Atheist, Crossway, 2004, pgs 46-48, 50

9 Lee Strobel, The Case For Faith, Zondervan, Grand Rapids, MI, 2000,pg 46

10 Ravi Zacharias, Jesus Among Other Gods, World Publishing, Nashville, 2000, Pg 114

11 Ravi Zacharias, Jesus Among Other Gods, World Publishing, Nashville, 2000, Pg 113

12 CS Lewis, Mere Christianity, Broadman & Holman, Nashville, 1996, pg 49

13 S Michael Houdmann, Why Does God Allow Evil?, Got Questions, monitored April 30, 2017,
https://www.gotquestions.org/God-allow-evil.html

14 Peter Bocchino, If God....Why Evil?, Legacy of Truth Ministries, viewed March 2002

15 Dr William Craig, Dr Craig's Opening Statement, Does God Exist, Craig / Nielson Debate, University of Western Ontario, Ontario, Canada, ReasonableFaith.Org, February 1991

16 Rich Deem, There is Too Much Evil and Suffering For God to Exist?

17 Richard Dawkins as quoted by Ravi Zacharias, Lessons From War in a Battle of Ideas, posted November 10, 2000

18 Philip Johnson, The Unraveling of Scientific Materialism, First Things, November 1997

19 Philip Johnson, Is God Constitutional?, University of California at Berkley, 1996, http://www.arn.org/docs/johnson/unconst1.htm

20 Dr Stephen Meyer, Does God Exist (DVD), True U, Truth Project, Focus on the Family, Part 2

21 THE EXPANDING UNIVERSE AND HUBBLE'S LAW, The Physics of the Universe, http://www.physicsoftheuniverse.com/topics_bigbang_expanding.html, 2009

22 Norman L Geisler & Frank Turek, I Don't Have Enough Faith to Be an Atheist, Crossway, 2004, pg73-74

23 THE EXPANDING UNIVERSE AND HUBBLE'S LAW, The Physics of the Universe, http://www.physicsoftheuniverse.com/topics_bigbang_expanding.html, 2009

24 Norman L Geisler & Frank Turek, I Don't Have Enough Faith to Be an Atheist, Crossway, 2004, pg 79

25 Chuck Missler, Atheism Hits a Brick Wall: The First Law of Thermodynamics, http://www.bibleprobe.com/thermodynamics.htm, Viewed February 6, 2015

26 Dr Philip Johnson, The Religion of the Blind Watchmaker, University of California at Berkley, 1996, http://www.arn.org/docs/johnson/watchmkr.htm

27 Elizabeth Howell, How Many Stars Are in the Milky Way?, Space.com, May 21, 2014

28 Robert Jastrow, God And The Astronomers, Chapter 1, WW Norton & Company, 1978, Viewed at http://www.unfitnews.com/authors/RJga1InBeginning.html

29 Robert Jastrow, God And The Astronomers, Chapter 6, WW Norton & Company, 1978, Viewed at http://www.unfitnews.com/authors/RJga1InBeginning.html

30 Gerald Scrhroeder, The Science of God, The Free Press, 1997, pgs 179-182

31 Scott Youngren, ON THE BIBLE AND FAIRY TALES…ATHEIST FAIRY TALES, Godevidence.com, September 3, 2013

32 The Universe: Evidence for Its Fine Tuning, www.godandscience.org/apologetics/designun.html, May 17, 2011

33 Gerald Scrhroeder, The Science of God, The Free Press, 1997

34 Gerald Scrhroeder, The Science of God, The Free Press, 1997, pg 5

35 H Margenau, & RA Varghese, Cosmos, Bios, and Theos. Open Court, 1992 pg 83

36 JN Willford, Sizing up the Cosmos: An Astronomers Quest. New York Times, March 12, 1991

37 Violence in the Cosmos, www.godandscience.org/love/sld024.html, updated March 31, 2008

38 God Proclaims His Love: Design of our Solar System, Godandscience.org/apologetics/designhtml,

39 The Incredible Design of the Earth and Our Solar System, www.godandscience.org/apologetics/designss.htm

40 George Greenstein, The Symbiotic Universe, William Morrow, 1989, pg 27

41 A Practical Man's Proof of God - Does God Exist?, www.doesgodexist.org/Pamphlets/Mansproof.htm

42 Frank Tipler, The Physics of Immortality, Doubleday, 1994, Preface

43 Creation Misquotes, http://www.huecotanks.com/debunk/misquote.htm, Viewed February 24, 2015

44 Richard Lewontin, Billions and Billions of Demons, Review of Carl Sagan's: The Demon-Haunted World: Science as a Candle in the Dark, New York Review of Books, January 9, 1997

45 The 7 Characteristics of Life, http:// infohost. nmt. edu/~klathrop/7characterisitcs_of_life.htm, Viewed February 24, 2015

46 Jerry Bergman, Why the Miller–Urey research argues against abiogenesis, Creation.com, Viewed February 24, 2015 Bergman cites his source as: "Poundstone, W., Carl Sagan; A Life in the Cosmos, Henry Holt, New York, 1999.

47 Jerry Bergman, Why the Miller–Urey research argues against abiogenesis, Creation.com, Viewed February 24, 2015

48 Don Batten, Origin of Life, Creation.com, November 26, 2013

49 Yockey, H., Information Theory and Molecular Biology, Cambridge University Press, 1992, p. 257 – As quoted by: Don Batten, Origin of Life, Creation.com, November 26, 2013

50 Quoted in, Evolution's final frontiers, New Scientist 201(2693):42, 2009: As quoted by Don Batten, Origin of Life, Creation.com, November 26, 2013

51 Bill Gates, The Road Ahead, Penguin: London, Revised, 1996, pg 228

52 Francis S. Collins, director of the Human Genome Project, The Language of God, (Free Press, New York, NY), 2006, p 1.

53 Mario Seigle, DNA: The Tiny Code That's Toppling Evolution, Good News Magazine, June 2005

54 Perry Marshall, Where Did the Universe Come From? Was it started by… God?, http://cosmicfingerprints.com/, Viewed February 25, 2015

55 Is God Real, http://www.everystudent.com/wires/Godreal.html, Viewed February 25, 2015

56 Lee Strobel, The Case for a Creator, Zondervan, 2004, pg 244

57 Harvard cracks DNA storage, crams 700 terabytes of data into a single gram, Extremetech.com, August 17, 2012

58 Michael Denton, Evolution a Theory in Crisis, Burnett Books, 1996, pg 329

59 Werner Gitt as quoted by: Mario Seigle, DNA: The Tiny Code That's Toppling Evolution, Good News Magazine, June 2005

60 Famous Atheist Now Believes in God, AP, December 9, 2004

61 Lee Strobel, The Case for a Creator, Zondervan, 2004, pg 221

62 Mario Seigle, DNA: The Tiny Code That's Toppling Evolution, Good News Magazine, June 2005

63 Margenau, H. and R. A. Varghese, eds. Cosmos, Bios, Theos: Scientists Reflect on Science, God, and the Origins of the Universe, Life, and Homo Sapiens (Open Court Pub. Co., La Salle, IL, 1992)

64 Robert Locke, The Scientific Case Against Evolution, Front Page Magazine, 2001

65 Norman L Geisler & Frank Turek, I Don't Have Enough Faith to Be an Atheist, Crossway, 2004, pg 140

66 Casey Luskin, What Are the Top Ten Problems with Darwinian Evolution?, Evolution News, July 12, 2012

67 John Michael Fischer, Debunking Evolution: Problems between the theory and reality, New Geology, 2005-2015

68 Molly K Burke, Joseph P. Dunham, Parvin Shahrestani, Kevin R Thornton, Michael R Rose, Anthony D Long, Genome-wide analysis of a long-term evolution experiment with Drosophila. Nature, Vol. 467, September 30, 2010 pgs 587-590

69 John Michael Fischer, Debunking Evolution: Problems between the theory and reality, New Geology, 2005-2015

70 Norman L Geisler & Frank Turek, I Don't Have Enough Faith to Be an Atheist, Crossway, 2004, pg 141

71 Charles Darwin, The Origin of Species, Penguin, 1958, pg 171

72 Michael Behe, Darwin's Black Box, Free Press, 1996, pg 39

73 Robert Locke, The Scientific Case Against Evolution, Front Page Magazine, 2001

74 Robert Locke, The Scientific Case Against Evolution, Front Page Magazine, 2001

75 Dr Ray Bohlin, Darwin's Black Box: The Biochemistry of the Cell, Probe Ministries, May 27, 1997 https://www.probe.org/darwins-black-box/

76 Michael Behe, Darwin's Breakdown: Irreducible Complexity & Design at the Foundation of Life, 4 Touchstone Magazine, July/Aug 1999

77 Dr Ray Bohlin, Darwin's Black Box: The Biochemistry of the Cell, Probe Ministries, May 27, 1997 https://www.probe.org/darwins-black-box/

78 Norman L Geisler & Frank Turek, I Don't Have Enough Faith to Be an Atheist, Crossway, 2004, pg 145

79 Norman L Geisler & Frank Turek, I Don't Have Enough Faith to Be an Atheist, Crossway, 2004, pg 148

80 General Rebuttal to the Theory of Evolution, www.godandscience.org/evolution/evolution.html, June 27, 2007

81 Gerald Schroeder, The Science of God, The Free Press, New York, 1997, pgs 88-89

82 Robert F DeHaan & John L Wiester, The Cambrian Explosion- The Fossil Evidence and Intelligent Design, Touchstone, July / August 1999

83 Gerald Schroeder, The Science of God, The Free Press, New York, 1997, pg 95

84 Robert Locke, The Scientific Case Against Evolution, Front Page Magazine, 2001

85 Robert Locke, The Scientific Case Against Evolution, Front Page Magazine, 2001

86 William A Dembski, What Every Theologian Should Know About Creation, Evolution and Design, Discovery, April 1, 1996

87 Denton was quoted from: Robert Locke, The Scientific Case Against Evolution, Front Page Magazine, 2001

88 Dr Ray Bohlin, Mere Creation: Science Faith and Intelligent Design, Probe Ministries, May 27, 2000

89 Curt Sewell, Some Arguments Favoring Creation, Creation Bits Number 4, November 2, 1999

90 Robert Locke, The Scientific Case Against Evolution, Front Page Magazine, 2001

91 Margenau, H and R.A. Varghese. Cosmos, Bios, and Theos. La Salle, IL, Open Court, 1993 pg 83

92 Robert Locke, The Scientific Case Against Evolution, Front Page Magazine, 2001

93 Paul E Little, Know Why You Believe, Chariot Victor, 1999, pgs 53-59

94 Don Closson, The Christian Canon, Probe Ministries International, 1996

95 Lee Strobel, The Case For Christ, Zondervan, 1998, pgs 86-90

96 How Do We Know Christianity Is True, Biblestudy.org

97 Lee Strobel, The Case For Christ, Zondervan, 1998, pg 76

98 Grant R Jeffrey, Jesus: The Great Debate, Frontier Research Publications, 1999, pgs 59-60

99 How Do We Know Christianity Is True, Biblestudy.org

100 Lee Strobel, The Case For Christ, Zondervan, 1998, pgs 83-85

101 Lee Strobel, The Case For Faith, Zondervan, 2000, pgs 83-85

102 Paul E Little, Know Why You Believe, Chariot Victor, 1999, pgs 78-85

103 Lee Strobel, The Case For Christ, Zondervan, 1998, pgs 130-132

104 Paul E Little, Know Why You Believe, Chariot Victor, 1999, pgs 76-77

105 Lee Strobel, The Case For Christ, Zondervan, 1998, pgs 132-133

106 Grant Jeffrey, The Great Debate, Frontier Research, 1999, pgs 84-91

107 Lee Strobel, The Case For Christ, Zondervan, 1998, pgs 40-44 & pg 66

108 Grant Jeffrey, The Great Debate, Frontier Research, 1999, pgs 50-54

109 Grant Jeffrey, The Great Debate, Frontier Research, 1999, pgs 173-174

110 Ofri Ilani, Dead Sea tablet suggests Jewish resurrection imagery pre-dates Jesus, Haaretz, July 6, 2008

111 Babylonian Talmud, Sanhedrin 98

112 Rashi (Rabbi Shlomo Yitzchaki), Jewish Virtual Library

113 Joel C Rosenberg, Missiles & The Messiah Making News, July 8,2008

114 Ancient Tablet Ignites Debate on Messiah and Resurrection, New York Times, July 6, 2008

115 Joel C Rosenberg, Missiles & The Messiah Making News, July 8,2008

116 Ancient Tablet Ignites Debate on Messiah and Resurrection, New York Times, July 6, 2008

117 Wendy Griffin, Messianic Revival In Israel?, CBN, July 13, 2008

118 Paul E Little, Know Why You Believe, Chariot Victor, 1999, pg 53-59

119 Grant Jeffrey, The Great Debate, Frontier Research, 1999, pg 229-239

120 Paul E Little, Know Why You Believe, Chariot Victor, 1999, pg 55

121 Grant Jeffrey, The Great Debate, Frontier Research, 1999, pg 229-239

122 Grant Jeffrey, The Great Debate, Frontier Research, 1999, pgs 162-164 & 184-188

123 Lee Strobel, The Case For Christ, Zondervan, 1998, pg 103-106

124 Grant Jeffrey, The Great Debate, Frontier Research, 1999, pg 166-168

125 Paul E Little, Know Why You Believe, Chariot Victor, 1999, pg 55

126 Jameel, Until Shiloh Comes, from The Timing of Messiah's First Coming, The Stillwater Trust, monitored September 2002

127 Grant Jeffrey, The Great Debate, Frontier Research, 1999, pg 193-213

128 Dr Mark Eastman, Daniel's Prophecy Came True When Yeshua Entered Jerusalem, Messianic Times, April 1996

129 John MacArthur Study Bible, notes to Matthew 2:1, pg 1,394

130 Sir Robert Anderson, The Coming Prince

131 Chuck Missler, Confirming the Prophetic Date of 445 BC, taken from the book: Mark Eastman, M.D. and Chuck Missler, The Creator Beyond Space and Time, 1996, The Word For Today. p.138,140-141

132 Dr Mark Eastman, Daniel"s Prophecy Came True When Yeshua Entered Jerusalem, Messianic Times, April 1996

133 Chuck Missler, Confirming The Prophetic Date of 445 BC, from Mark Eastman, M.D. and Chuck Missler,

134 Sir Robert Anderson, The Coming Prince, 1881

135 Dr Mark Eastman, Daniel's Prophecy Came True When Yeshua Entered Jerusalem, Messianic Times, April 1996

136 Steve Brown, The Sure Things In Life, Key Life Ministries, monitored 2001

137 araslav Pelikan, The Illustrated Jesus Through The Centuries, Yale University Press, 1997, pg 9-23

138 Professor LT Jeyachandran, The Person of Christ, Peace Ministry, viewed 2001

139 Norman Geisler & Peter Bocchino, Unshakeable Foundations, Bethany House, Minneapolis, 2001, pg 296-297

140 Norman Geisler & Peter Bocchino, Unshakeable Foundations, Bethany House, Minneapolis, 2001, pg 287-288

141 Paul E Little, Know Why You Believe, Chariot Victor, 1999, pg 36

142 Norman Geisler & Peter Bocchino, Unshakeable Foundations, Bethany House, Minneapolis, 2001, pg 303-304

143 Lee Strobel, The Case For Christ, Zondervan, 1998, pg 308-309

144 Josh McDowell, Evidence For The Resurrection, Leadership U, 1992

145 Josh McDowell, Evidence For The Resurrection, Leadership U, 1992

146 David Cloud, Way of Life Literature, April 4, 2017

147 John MacArthur Why One Way?, W Publishing Group, Pg 7- 9

148 Keith E Johnson, Do All Paths Lead to the Same Destination, Leaderu.com

149 Fritz Ridenour, So What's the Difference, Regal Books, Ventura, 2001, pg 94

150 Gannon Murphy, Do All Paths Lead to God?, Geocities, monitored 2000

151 Ravi Zacharias, ON Truth, Gospel.com, monitored 2000

152 Norman Geisler & Peter Bocchino, Unshakeable Foundations,Bethany House, 2001, pg 296-297

153 Keith E Johnson, Do All Paths Lead to the Same Destination, Leaderu.com

154 Fritz Ridenour, So What's the Difference, Regal Books, Ventura, 2001, pg 89-96

155 Fritz Ridenour, So What's the Difference, Regal Books, Ventura, 2001,pg 104-106

156 Fritz Ridenour, So What's the Difference, Regal Books, Ventura, 2001, pg 151-160

157 Fritz Ridenour, So What's the Difference, Regal Books, Ventura, 2001, Pg 79-86

158 Timothy George, Is the Father of Jesus The God of Muhammed?, Breakpoint, October 23, 2001

159 Grant Jeffrey, Jesus: The Great Debate, Frontier Publications, 1999, pg 273

160 CS Lewis, Mere Christianity, Broadman & Holman, 1996, pg 64

161 STUDY: ONE-FIFTH OF JEWISH MILLENNIALS BELIEVE JESUS IS THE SON OF GOD, Jerusalem Post, November 1, 2017

162 The Rabbi, the Note and the Messiah, Israel Today, May 30,2013

CPSIA information can be obtained
at www.ICGtesting.com
Printed in the USA
FFOW02n1311060118
44374034-44089FF